MiG-19 Farmer

in action

By Hans-Heiri Stapfer

Color by Don Greer and Tom Tullis

Illustrated by Joe Sewell

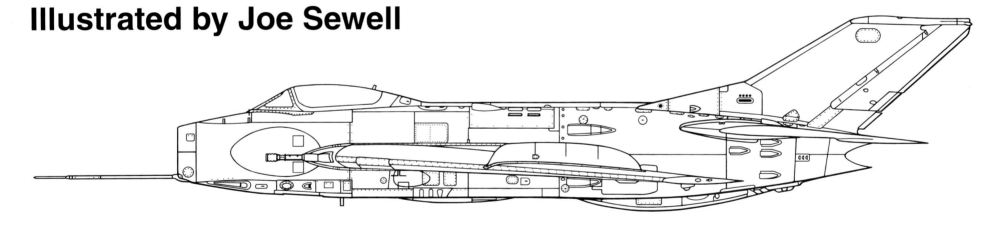

Aircraft Number 143

squadron/signal publications

FLT LT K. Latif, flying a Chinese-built F-6 (MiG-19S) Farmer C shot down an Indian Air Force Sukhoi Su-7 Fitter on 4 December 1971 during the 1971 Indian/Pakistani war. On this day, Pakistani pilots claimed a total of ten Indian aircraft destroyed and four damaged.

Dedication

Well folks; initially I had decided to dedicate this book to Csilla, the most impressive girl I had ever met in Hungary. She had a lot of fantastic advantages; her mother was an excellent cook, her father owned a Palinka brandy distillery and she lived in Budapest, one of the most beautiful cities I have ever seen. So what more could you want to have paradise on earth?

Sadly the odds and Csilla were against me as I finally discovered during my last trip to Budapest. But, without Csilla, my (night) life really started to grow. I immediately fell in love with Palinka (the Hungarian equivalent of American Whisky or Russian Vodka) and in fact, this is the most outstanding beverage I have had in recent years. So my advice to everyone, just in case you will write a book; never dedicate it to any woman, better dedicate it to your best friends, your favorite beer, your favorite heavy metal band — but never to a girl!

COPYRIGHT 1994 SQUADRON/SIGNAL PUBLICATIONS, INC.
1115 CROWLEY DRIVE CARROLLTON, TEXAS 75011-5010
All rights reserved. No part of this publication may be reproduced, stored in a retrieval system or transmitted in any form by means electrical, mechanical or otherwise, without written permission of the publisher.

ISBN 0-89747-311-6

If you have any photographs of aircraft, armor, soldiers or ships of any nation, particularly wartime snapshots, why not share them with us and help make Squadron/Signal's books all the more interesting and complete in the future. Any photograph sent to us will be copied and the original returned. The donor will be fully credited for any photos used. Please send them to:

Squadron/Signal Publications, Inc.
1115 Crowley Drive.
Carrollton, TX 75011-5010

Acknowledgments and Photo Credits

Peter Steinemann
Pavel Polach
Daniel Keller
Klaus Meissner
Hadtorteneti Museum
Dusan Mikolas
David Oliver
Dick Cole
Oleg V. Luzenko
A. A. Zirnov
Andrzej Morgala
Hans-Georg Volprich
Tibor Sinka
Dave Hatherell
Bernard Denes
Wojoiech Luczak
Saverio "Usus" Sepe
Jim Walg
Andras Nagy
Nicholas J. Waters III

Achille Vigna
Jens Schymura
Viktor K. Kabanov
T. Galfe
Marii Chernev
Jeri Vrany
Johann Sauberzweig
Martin Kyburz
Viktor Kulikow
Prof. Jan Beranek
Jordan Andreev
Dirk Kahle
Attila Bonhardt
Helmut Kluger
Air Forces Monthly Magazine
Simon Watson
MiG Design Bureau
Mariusz Konarski
Zolnierz Polski

Robert Bock
Martin Baumann
Wolfgang Tamme
George Punka
Zdenek Titz
Dan Antoniu
Roman Sekyrka
Pavel Simek
Josef Simon
Marcus Fulber
Hans-Joachim Mau
Andreas Schutz
Zdenek Hurt
Martin Dorsky
Alain Pelletier
Viktor K. Kabanov
Andor Gibas
Paul Jackson

The MiG-19 Farmer was the world's first operational supersonic fighter. The MiG-19 had an impressive thrust to weight ratio and an outstanding rate of climb making it a formidable interceptor and dog-fighter. This Farmer C was a Czech-built S-105 (MiG-19S). (Pavel Simek via Pavel Polach)

Introduction

The MiG-19 was the ultimate in the line of swept wing fighters designed and built by the MiG Design Bureau, although it was not produced in the same numbers as the MiG-15 and MiG-17 nor did it remain in front line service for an extended period. The MiG-19 was viewed as an interim fighter developed and built to meet the threat presented by Western supersonic fighters being produced during the early 1950s.

The MiG-19 was, in many ways, an outstanding aircraft. It was not only the first mass produced supersonic fighter the world, it also had a fantastic rate of climb, which was not matched by any other Western contemporary design. When compared with its American contemporary, the North American F-100 Super Sabre, the first Western supersonic fighter, the MiG-19 clearly possessed advantages in rate of climb, level speed and landing characteristics.

For a short time, the Soviet Union not only reached Western standards, it even surpassed its competitors west of the Iron Curtain. This was a truly great achievement considering the fact that the Soviet aviation industry was years behind American, British and German standards at the end of the Great Patriotic War in May of 1945.

Due to the fast pace of aviation progress in the mid-1950s, supersonic fighter designs were quickly overtaken by Mach 2 capable fighters being developed on both sides of the Iron Curtain. The MiG-19 was regarded by the Soviets as an interim solution until the MiG-21 Fishbed became available. In the West, the F-100 and the French Super Mystere B2 met the same fate, being quickly replaced by Mach 2 designs such as the F-104 and Mirage III.

Regardless of the fact that the MiG-19 was only built in limited numbers when compared with other post-war MiG designs, it saw a considerable amount of combat. During the Vietnam war, the Farmer was respected by USAF crews flying aircraft of much newer design. Due to its maneuverability and outstanding rate of climb, the Vietnamese MiG-19 became a deadly threat for American air crews in Southeast Asia. In the Middle East, MiG-19s and F-6s were used by various Arab Air Forces against the Israeli Air Force. In the Indian/Pakistani conflict, Chinese-built F-6s of the Pakistani Air Force were involved in clashes with the Farmer's successor, the MiG-21 Fishbed flown by Indian Air Force pilots. Pakistani Air Force F-6s did score a number of victories over the Indians. Soviet MiG-19s were responsible for shooting down a USAF RB-66C over the German Democratic Republic during 1964. On 1 May 1955, Farmers were involved in the interception of Gary Powers' U-2; which was subsequently shot down by SAMs near Sverdlovsk. Chinese F-6s have also downed various intruders over their homeland.

Project SM-1 (I-340)

In 1950, the first sketches were laid down at the MiG Design Bureau for a fighter aircraft which would fly faster than the speed of the sound, with a greater range than any other fighter type previously produced by this design bureau. The SM-1 was the beginning of an experimental program for a twin engined supersonic fighter that later evolved into the MiG-19 Farmer. The MiG OKB (*Opyto Konstruktorskoe Byuro*/Experimental Design Bureau) began in mid-1950 a program aimed at producing a fighter design that would permit sustained supersonic speeds in level flight without undue piloting difficulties.

The MiG-15LL and some experimental MiG-17s had been able to reach the speed of sound for brief periods, but neither could maintain Mach 1 for an extended period. The research phase of the design was carried out in close co-operation with TsAGI (*Tsentral'ny Aerogidrodinamicheski Institut* or Central Aero and Hydrodynamics Institute) and the TsIAM (*Tsential'nyi Institut Aviatsionnovo Motorostroeniya* or Central Aero Engine Institute).

While airframe research was ongoing, the Alexander Mikulin Design Bureau was working on the AM-5, a single shaft turbojet engine. This engine was hampered by teething troubles at the beginning, but it was regarded as the only suitable engine available to power a supersonic fighter due to a number of factors, including its small diameter and, by Soviet standards, excellent fuel consumption.

For the first time the MiG Design Bureau had chosen a twin engine layout for an interceptor fighter. The AM-5 engine would allow the fighter to fly at sustained supersonic speeds and, thanks to its lower fuel consumption, it would also have a much longer range that current fighter types in service with the Soviet Air Force. In order to test the proposed side-by-side engine configuration of the new fighter, a standard MiG-17 Fresco A was converted to this configuration. The aircraft began flight testing during late 1951 with Grigorij A. Sedov at the controls. It was equipped with two AM-5s, which were soon replaced by improved AM-5A engines. Even without afterburners, the thrust of the two AM-5As was more than the thrust of the standard VK-1F afterburning turbojet used in the MiG-17F, while the weight of the two engines was only 194 pounds (88 kg) more than the single VK-1F.

Trials with an SM-1 prototype fitted with two AM-5As were carried out at the test and experimental center at Zhukovsky, some 35 miles southeast of Moscow. These tests revealed that the SM-1 was under powered and it was decided to fit the aircraft with two new AM-5F afterburning engines, each rated at 4,739 lbst (2,150 kg) dry and 5,952 lbst (2,700 kg) in afterburner. In addition to installing the new engines, MiG also made a number of other changes to the technology-demonstrator. Two addition fuel cells, one of 58.1 gallons (220 liters) and one of 87.1 gallons (330 liters) were installed in the fuselage along with a container in the rear fuselage for a braking parachute.

Data obtained from the factory tests at Zhukovsky helped prove that the side-by-side configuration of the engines was practical and laid the ground work for an improved twin engine fighter prototype. But at the same time it was noted that the thrust of the two AM-5Fs was still insufficient to power a truly supersonic fighter. During these trials the SM-1 attained a speed of 741 mph (1,193 kmh) at 16,400 feet (5,000 meters) and displayed a rate of climb of

The SM-1 was a prototype of a twin engined supersonic fighter aircraft developed from the MiG-17 Fresco A during late 1951. Initially, the SM-1 was powered by two AM-5 A engines, which were later replaced by afterburning AM-5F engines. (MiG Design Bureau)

The SM-2/1 prototype shortly before it began flight testing at the Zhukovsky Test Center during April of 1952. The prototype carried a 200 gallon (760 liter) drop tank, had a MiG-15 type ejection seat, a trim tab on the rudder and a RV-2 radio antenna on the rear fuselage. (MiG Design Bureau)

over 8,000 feet per minute. There was only one SM-l built and it was given the military designation I-340 (I for Istrebitel or Fighter).

Project SM-2 (I-360)

On 30 July 1950, Iosif Stalin held a meeting in the Kremlin on the subject of future combat aircraft for the Soviet Air Force. One of the main concerns was that this new generation of combat aircraft have a longer range than the aircraft currently in production. The MiG Design Bureau was entrusted to work on a modified version of the well proved MiG-17 Fresco with an increased range (which would evolve into the MiG-19). Yakovlev, who was also at this meeting, received an order to proceed with the Yak-25 Flashlight twin engined, long range, all-weather, radar equipped fighter.

MiGs new project was given the company designator SM-2 and the military designation I-360. The project was under the leadership of General Designer Anatolij G. Brunov, while his deputy, Rostislav A. Belyakov directed all the various departments within the MiG OKB involved with the various sub-systems on the new aircraft.

The new designed featured a 55 degree swept wing, which incorporated an N-37D 37MM cannon in each wing root. The armament team, under N. Volkov, was responsible for the arrangement of the weapons and their ammunition in the wing. The advantage of the wing root layout was that it saved space within the nose for other equipment.

The SM-2 differed from the earlier SM-1 in that the fuselage was lengthened by 5.25 feet (1.6 meters), the wing span was decreased from 31.5 feet (9.62 m) to 29.6 feet (9.04 m) and overall weight increased from 11,486 pounds (5,210 kg) to 15,035 pounds (6,820 kg). The SM-1 wing had three wing fences (standard MiG-17 wing), while the SM-2 had only a single wing fence. The landing light was repositioned from the underside of the port wing to under the nose. The main landing gear was also modified and the gear doors changed. The ventral fin under the rear fuselage was enlarged to increase the aircraft's side area. The aircraft also featured a high mounted T type horizontal stabilizer.

The first improved SM-2/1 left the MiG experimental shop in April of 1952, and began flight testing on 24 May. The aircraft could only reach high subsonic speeds, until the AM-5F engines were installed, then the aircraft was able to reach speeds of up to Mach 1.19. This prototype was followed by a second, the SM-2/2 which differed mainly in armament details (short vs long barrel cannon) and in that it could not carry the 200 gallon drop tanks used on the SM-2/1. Both testbeds were used for factory and state test pilots during the evaluation phase of the flight test program. One of the most serious flaws in the SM-2s was the high mounted T tail. This caused at least one serious incident in which one prototype was nearly lost. As a result, the horizontal tail surfaces were relocated to the fuselage and their area was increased. The vertical fin was also redesigned with a larger rudder area. After these and other detail changes were made, the designation of the prototypes was changed to SM-2 and SM-2A. Later the wing fences were enlarged on the SM-2A and the designation changed to SM-2B. In the Summer of 1953, both aircraft were turned over for state acceptance trials.

While the state acceptance trials found that the engine arrangement was satisfactory, there were a number of shortcomings in the design that needed to be worked out before the aircraft could be cleared for production. As a result the two prototypes were rebuilt to serve as pattern aircraft for the production standard fighter. Eventually, they emerged from the experimental shop with new engines (AM-9Bs) and a new designation, the SM-9/1 and SM-9/2. The AM-9B engines offered a increase in power of some 1,212 lbst (550kg). To accommodate the new engines the rear fuselage was redesigned and new cooling air intakes were added at various points on the rear fuselage

The SM-9/1 flew for the first time on 5 January 1954, and on its second flight the prototype exceeded Mach 1 in level flight. During this period the armament was changed. The two 37MM cannon in the wing roots were changed to NR-23 23MM cannon and a single N-37D 37MM cannon was added to the underside of the starboard nose section. Additionally, a BD-3-56 underwing pylon was added to each wing to allow the aircraft to carry 200 gallon (760 liter) drop tanks. The SM-9/2 was rebuilt with a longer nose section and test flown.

Flight tests revealed that the SM-9/1 was 236 mph (380 kmh) faster than the MiG-17F and had a service ceiling some 2,952 feet (900m) better than the Fresco C.

The SM-9/2 had a stretched non-standard nose and the gun camera was placed almost inside the air intake. The large gun blast panels were retained, but no armament was carried. The SM-9/2 differed from the SM-9/1 in that it had two frames in the canopy. (Yefim Gordon)

The SM-9/1 prototype had the engine exhausts modified to Farmer A standards during factory testing in January of 1954. In this stage the SM-9/1 carried an armament of two N-37D 37MM cannon in the wing roots and the aircraft did not carry an SRD-1M range finder on the nose. (Yefim Gordon)

Development

SM 9/1

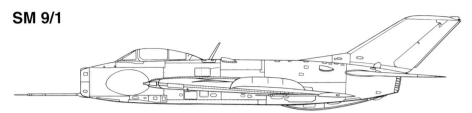

SM-9/2

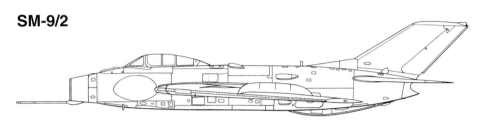

MiG-19 Farmer A

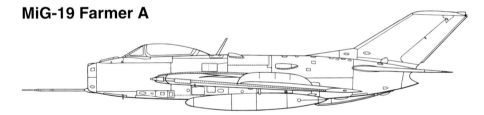

MiG-19S Farmer C

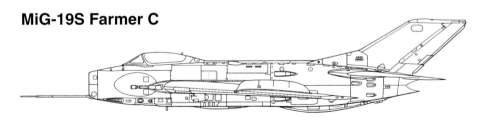

MiG-19P Farmer B

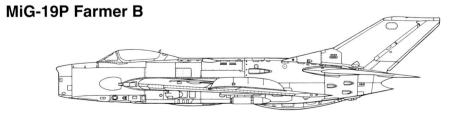

MiG-19PM Farmer E

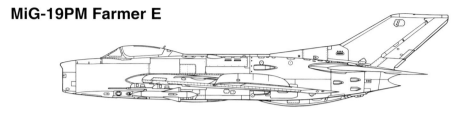

Shenyang J-6 (Early)

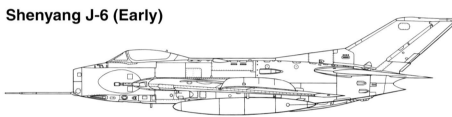

Shenyang F-6

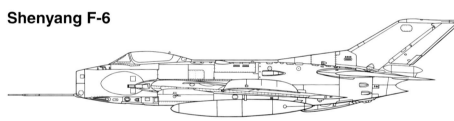

Shenyang F-6 (Pakistani Mod)

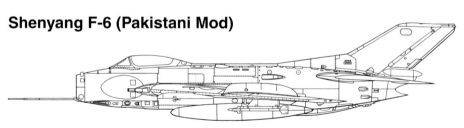

Shenyang TF-6

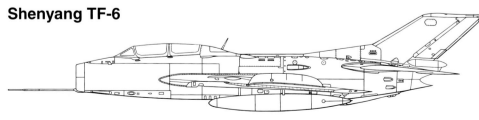

MiG-19 Farmer A

With most of the shortcomings of the SM-2 prototype eliminated, the aircraft was ordered into production by the MAP (*Ministerstvo Aviatsionnoi Promyshlennostil* or Ministry for Aircraft Production) under the public designation MiG-19 on 17 February 1954. The MAP designation for the MiG-19 was "Type 25". The designation MiG-19 was only for public use, while the "Type 25" designation appeared on the official production lists and other documents.

At this time the SM-9/1 prototype had not passed either its factory test trials or the state acceptance trials. The order to put the aircraft into production prior to completing the testing cycle reflected the Soviet Air Force's urgent need for a supersonic interceptor fighter. With production initiated, the USSR became the first nation to have a supersonic fighter in production and in service.

The initial production order issued by the Ministry of Aircraft production included fifty aircraft to be built at GAZ-21 (*Gosudarstvenny Aviatsionny Zavod* or State Aircraft Factory) at Nizhny-Novgorod and GAZ-153, the "*Valery Chkalov*" plant at Novosibirsk. GAZ-21 was established before the Second World War and had built Polikarpov I-16s as well LaGG-3s during the war while GAZ-153 had been established during the war as a Yak-7 and Yak 9 production plant. GAZ-153 was named in honor of the famous Soviet aviator Valery Chkalov.

The first MiG-19s were delivered to the Frontal Air Forces Regiments in March of 1955, barely fourteen months after the maiden flight of the SM-9. The new type was introduced to the public during the Air Parade over Tushino Air Base near Moscow on 3 July 1955. This was also the first time Western observers noted the new supersonic fighter and NATO allocated the ASCC-Reporting Name Farmer A to the new fighter.

The SM-9 (SM-2) series of prototypes led directly to the MiG-19 Farmer A. Once testing with the SM-9s was completed the type was ordered into production under the designation MiG-19 on 17 February 1954. (Yefim Gordon)

Due to the fact that the Soviet Union did not release any information on the manufacturer and the designation on the Farmer A at the time of the Air Parade, there was much speculation in the West regarding the technical details, dimensions and manufacturer. A number of false and speculative designations appeared in contemporary Western aviation magazines, such as MiG-21, Yak-25 and ZAGI-418. Nearly a year later, on 24 June 1956, a large formation MiG-19 Farmer As were displayed again over Tushino during the traditional air display alongside a number of Yakovlev Yak-25 Flashlight interceptors.

There were a number of differences between the SM-9/l and the production MiG-19 Farmer A. While the SM-9/1 and SM-9/2 both carried a large gun blast panel (a carry over from the SM-2 configuration) this panel was deleted on all production Farmer As. The original armament of the SM-9/1 consisted of two N-37D cannons in the wing roots, while the production MiG-19 had two NR-23 cannon in the wing roots with the gun barrels being covered by a conical aerodynamic alloy tube. A N-37D cannon was carried on the lower starboard nose section of the fuselage with a gun blast panel in front of it and a shell ejection port was added behind the cannon.

The SM 9/1 had a two piece rear canopy with reinforcing frames, while production versions deleted these frames. Additionally, the rear portion of the canopy glazing was redesigned to give the pilot a better view to the rear. The SM 9/1 featured wing tip pitot tubes and these were deleted on the production Farmer A. A Syrena 2 tail warning radar antenna was added above the position light on the fin on the Farmer A and a SRD-1 "Konus" range finder, which had been deleted on the SM 9/1, was reintroduced on the Farmer A. The SRD-1M range finder feed the ASP-4N gunsight and had a maximum usable distance of 6,417 feet. Most serial MiG-19s also carried a small aerial slightly behind the port nose wheel door. The Farmer A also had a small pitot tube added on the starboard side in front of the canopy. This tube was not fitted on the either the SM-2 or SM-9 prototypes.

Fuselage Development

SM-9/2 Prototype (Modified)

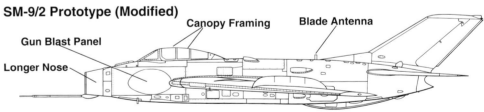

MiG-19 Farmer A

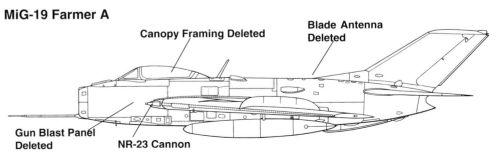

A MiG-19 Farmer A, Blue 26, on an operational Soviet Air Force base. The tactical number has a thin small outline. The Farmer A differed from the SM-9 prototypes in that the frame on the rear sliding canopy was deleted and the rear portion redesigned. Additionally, the first prototype lacked the pitot tube fitted to the starboard side of the nose (just above the tactical number) on all production Farmer As. (A.A. Zirnov)

The MiG-19 Farmer A was the first MiG fighter equipped with a braking parachute. The pneumatically released fourteen foot five inch (4.5 m) TF-19 drag chute was carried in a compartment in the lower rear portion of the port empennage. The drag chute reduced the landing run drastically from 2.625 feet (800 m/without chute) to 1,969 feet (600 m/with chute).

The fuselage of the MiG-19 Farmer A was a conventional stressed skin aluminum construction with the fuselage broken into two major assemblies. The forward section consisted of the air intake and associated ducting. The rear section, attached by four quick-release bolts, was easily removed at joint just to the rear of the wing trailing edge for power plant and related systems maintenance and support. The fuselage skinning around the engine exhaust nozzles was of heat resistant steel.

The MiG-19 Farmer A had a wingspan of thirty feet two inches (9.19 m). The wing was a highly swept single spar wing of primarily D-16-T aluminum alloy with leading edge sweep angle of 58 degrees, changing to 55 degrees at quarter chord. The ailerons were hydraulically-boosted and the Fowler type flaps were hydraulically actuated. The flaps had extension angles of fifteen degrees for take off and twenty-five degrees for landing. In contrast to the MiG-17 Fresco, which had three small wing fences on each wing, there was a single 12.57 inch high wing fence on each wing of the Farmer.

The landing gear consisted of a conventional, tricycle arrangement with free-castoring nose gear. The main gear retracted inward the toward fuselage centerline and were stored in wells aft of main wing spar. The nose gear retracted forward into a well built into the space between the air intake tunnels. Landing gear retraction and extension was hydraulic with a pneumatic emergency back up system for lowering the landing gear.,

A double redundant 3,000 pounds per square inch hydraulic system was provided and a power takeoff from the starboard engine provided the pressure to the system. The hydraulic system provided power to the landing gear, flaps, air brakes, exhaust nozzles, and also provided back up power to the flight control system. The port engine hydraulic unit provided-primary power for the flight control system. In case of the failure of one of the engines, the other AM-9B power plant automatically takes over the responsibilities of the lost engine.

Standard armament for the Farmer A included two NR-23 23MM cannons in the wing roots. These guns were developed by A. Nudelman and A.A. Richter and had a rate of fire of 850 rpm. The N-37D 37MM cannon in the starboard side of the nose had a rate of fire of 400 rpm. The aircraft could also carry a variety of bombs between 110 pound (50 kg) and 551 pounds (250 kg) on the BD-3-56 universal pylon in place of the standard 200 gallon (760 liter) drop tank. The aircraft could also be fitted with a small pylon on each wing undersurface behind the outer main wheel doors for an ORO-57K pod with eight S-5 unguided rockets. The two basic types of the S-5 rockets could be carried, the S-5M for air-to-air and the S-5K for ground attack duties.

There was also another armament layout evaluated on one MiG-19 Farmer A, Red 420. This aircraft was fitted with a pylon on the wing leading edge to carry a pod with four S-5 rockets. This type of pylon was never adopted on Soviet MiG-19s but the East German Air Force used the same kind of weapons pylon on their MiG-19 Farmer Cs, as did the Chinese on their F-6s. Another MiG-19, Red 406, was tested with unguided S-21 210MM rockets mounted in place of the underwing drop tank on special pylons.

Within Frontal Aviation and Air Defense Regiments the MiG-19 soon earned the reputation as a "widow maker". During the early phase of its operational service, several MiG-19 Farmer As and their pilots were lost because of in flight explosions of the aircraft. These explosions occurred so suddenly that the pilot could not inform ground control of his problem. It was later determined that the heat generated by the two side-by-side AM-5B power plants heated the rear fuel fuselage fuel tank, mounted below the engines, until it reached a point where the fuel exploded. This problem was solved by introducing a large heat-resistant metal plate between the fuel tank and the engine bays.

Additional looses were caused by the demanding flight characteristics of the Farmer A. When compared with the MiG-15 Fagot and MiG-17 Fresco, which were really "pilot's planes", the MiG-19 needed much more skill to be mastered. The major shortcoming; however, was low control surface effectiveness at supersonic speeds. The Farmer A had been pushed into mass production even with this well known shortcoming in order to provide the Soviet Air Force with a supersonic interceptor — at the ultimate cost to a number pilots.

A MiG-19 Farmer A shares the ramp with several Sukhoi Su-7BM Fitter As at a ground crew school outside of Moscow. The rear canopy of Blue 08 has been removed from the aircraft and, usual for this time period, the national markings are carried on the upper wing surface. (Yefim Gordon)

Super Sabre needed nearly four minutes to reach 34,448 feet (10,500m)! The top speed, climb rate and service ceiling of the MiG-19 Farmer A were all better than that of the North American F-100 Super Sabre, which flew some four month after the MiG. The Super Sabre also was also some 73 percent heavier than the MiG-19. For the first time in history, the Soviet Union had an interceptor in its inventory that had a superior performance to a American competitors design.

The MiG-19 was built for about a year at GAZ-21 at Nizhny-Novgorod and GAZ-153 at Novosibirsk in relatively low numbers before production switched for the more advanced MiG-19S Farmer C.

The MiG-19 Farmer A was only used in the Frontal Aviation and Air Defenses Regiments of the Soviet Air Force and with the arrival of sufficient number of MiG-19S Farmer C and later MiG-21F Fishbeds these early versions were transferred to training units within the Soviet Air Force or placed in storage depots within the Soviet Union. In sharp contrast to the later MiG-19S the Farmer A was never exported outside of the Soviet Union.

All MiG-19 Farmer A were delivered in an overall Natural Metal finish with the national markings applied on the wing undersurfaces and on the tail fin. There were a few Farmer As which had the national markings also applied on top of the wing. Combat units used two digit tactical numbers which were either not outlined or had a small Black outline. Aircraft with the tactical number 01 to 13 were allocated to the 1st squadron of a regiment, 20 to 31 were allocated to the 2nd squadron, while the 3rd squadron had tactical numbers from 40 to 51. A Red two digit tactical number denoted a Guards Regiment, while Blue tactical numbers were issued to units belonging to the PVO (Air Defense Regiments). Training units could be identified by larger three digit tactical numbers. In addition, experimental MiG-19 Farmer As allocated to the MiG Design Bureau also carried three digit Red tactical numbers with no outline.

A line-up of MiG-19 Farmer As on the ramp of a Soviet Air Force base. When parked, the large air data boom was always folded up to prevent damage by ground crews and vehicles. The tactical number in the 20 range denotes that all of these Farmer As belong to the 2nd Squadron and the Blue color denotes that they the regiment is assigned to the Air Defense Command. All of the Farmer As carry 200 gallon (760 liter) drop tanks. (A.A. Zirnov)

Another unpleasant handling characteristic was when using the two air brakes on the rear fuselage, the Farmer A tended to pitch up rather violently since a low pressure area formed behind the air brakes and the airflow pattern was shifted under the horizontal stabilizers.

On the positive side, the MiG-19 had a phenomenal rate of climb for its time. It only needed 1 minute 6 seconds to climb to 32,800 feet (10,000 m) and 3 minutes 30 seconds for 49,212 feet (15,000 m). Service ceiling was 57,414 feet (17,500 m) and the maximum speed at 32,800 feet (10,000 m) was 901.6 mph (1,451 kmh). With this extraordinary rate of climb the MiG-19 outclassed any contemporary Western interceptor. Its direct competitor, the F-100

A retired MiG-19 Farmer A in the storage yard at Kharkov Air Base in the Ukraine. The high tactical number would indicate that this aircraft's last assignment was advanced trainer. High numbers were usually given to two seat trainers and single seat training aircraft. This particular Farmer A still carries a ORO-57K pod for unguided S-5 rockets under the wing. (Yefim Gordon)

Project SM-10

Experimental in flight refueling variants of the MiG-15 Fagot-and MiG-17 Fresco had been built and tested and a project to give MiG-19 air-to-air refueling capability was also undertaken. In May of 1954, an government sponsored contract was submitted to the MiG Design Bureau ordering them to modify a Farmer A to test air-to-air refueling methods from the Tu-16N tanker version of the Badger A bomber. The man responsible for this project at the MiG OKB was A.I. Komissarov. The aim of the modification program was to increase the range of the MiG-19 beyond the normal 1,367 mile (2,200 km) range (when fitted with two 200 gallon tanks).

During mid-1955 work began on the in flight refueling version of the MiG-19 begun under the designation SM-10. A standard production Farmer A, Red 415, was modified with a refueling receptacle, similar to that of the Tu-22 Blinder bomber, mounted on the port wing tip. No armament was carried and an additional antenna was mounted on top of the rear fuselage. The oxygen capacity was increased to 18 liter on the SM-10.

The factory test trials started during the Autumn of 1955 at Zhukovsky and were under the leadership of MiG's chief test pilot Vladimir A. Nefyodov. The standard refueling procedure was that the SM-10 approached on the extreme right in same direction of flight as the tanker fitted with a house-and-drogue refueling system. Contact with the tanker's probe-and-drogue system was made at a speed of 280 to 310 mph (450 to 500 kmh). Once the contact was established, fuel flow began (normally about a 1,000 liters/minute fuel flow). Most of the refueling trials were made at an altitude of 29,500-32,000 feet (9,000 to 10,000 m). The receiver had to remember that it was important to approach the Tu-16 on the extreme right in

The SM-10 testbed, Red 415, was modified with a refueling probe from a Tu-22 Blinder on the port wing tip. The armament was deleted and an antenna was added above the nose wheel door and on top of the rear fuselage. Factory tests with the SM-10 and a Tu 16 tanker started in the Autumn of 1956. (MiG Design Bureau)

This MiG-19 Farmer A, Red 420, was modified with a weapons pylon mounted on the forward portion of the wing. This pylon was intended to carry a rocket pod containing four S-5 unguided rockets. This additional pylon was never adopted for service use by the Soviet Air Force, but the East Germans and Chinese fitted their Farmers with a similar pylon. (MiG Design Bureau)

same direction of flight in order to avoid turbulence from the tanker aircraft.

As soon the tanks were full the fuel flow was shut down and both aircraft separated. The refueling trials proved successful and some tests were even conducted at night with the aid of a searchlight mounted in the Tu-16N tanker.

After the factory tests had been successfully completed, the SM-10 was transferred to the Flight Research Institute or LII for state acceptance trials under the control of LII test pilot V.N. Pronyakin. The state acceptance trials lasted until 1956, when it became clear that the Soviet Air Force would not accept in flight refueling systems in its inventory due to a change in strategic requirements and serious defense budget cuts during the Khrushchev era.

It was decided by the leading Soviet generals that surface-to-surface and surface-to-air missile would fulfill the task better than the combination of tanker aircraft and interceptor aircraft and as a result the majority of defense expenditures were used for development of such missiles. One of the reasons for this was that it was not uncommon for manned Soviet interceptors to fail to intercept Western aircraft flying reconnaissance missions into Soviet and Eastern European airspace.

Project SM-30

In the mid-1950s there were several concepts for a zero-length-launcher (ZELL) for fighter aircraft worked out on both sides of the Iron Curtain. The idea was that a fighter aircraft was carried into battle on a trailer and literally blasted into the sky by the use of powerful RATO units. In this manner, fighters could be based in areas where no airfields were available or where runways had been destroyed by the enemy. Air bases proved to be a large and highly vulnerable target for enemy action.

An early predecessor of the ZELL idea was the Bachem Ba 349 Natter (Viper) developed by the Germans in the Second World War. Loaded with unguided rockets in the nose, the Ba 349 Natter was to be launched from a vertical ramp placed near the target the aircraft was defending. Large numbers of Ba 349 launchers would circle the area and be launched to intercept intruding American B-17 Flying Fortress and B-24 Liberator bomber before they could drop their loads. As with many sophisticated projects of the Third Reich, the Ba 349 did not develop beyond the testing stage.

The ZELL concept had been accepted by the Soviet High Command and in April of 1955, an order had been issued to the MiG Design Bureau to modify five MiG-19 Farmer As to test the concept under the designation Project SM-30.

Responsible for Project SM-30 was Mikhail I. Gurevich as general supervisor with chief-designer A.G. Agronik responsible for the conversion of the Farmer airframes.

In order to withstand the expected 4.5 Gs during a ZELL take off, the entire fuselage and wing structure of the SM-30 prototypes was strengthened. Some spars in the wing and fuselage were also strengthened as was the mountings of the Number Two and Three fuselage fuel tanks.

Instead of a single ventral fin, the SM-30 prototypes were modified with two side-by-side ventral fins of slightly smaller dimensions. The SRD-1M range finder was removed and an additional aerial was added under the nose. The ejection seat headrest was modified so that the pilot's head was held firm during the ZELL launch.

The thrust required for the ZELL take-off was provided by two PRD-22 solid propellant RATO units which were installed under the aircraft at a slight downward angle. The PRD-22 booster had been developed by the MiG Design Bureau under the leadership of I.I. Kartukov. It provided more than 80,000 pounds of thrust for 2.5 seconds. The thrust provided by the two PRD-22 was approximately five times the aircraft's gross weight.

The PU-30 mobile launcher was also developed by the MiG Design Bureau using a YaAZ-210 dual axle trailer as a base. The PU-30 trailer was capable of operating from virtually any surface capable of supporting its weight and a variety of levers and related equipment was permanently mounted to the primary structure. The launch rail itself was articulated and

One of the five SM-30s just as it lifts off the PU-30 launching trailer. The PRD-22 RATO units have fired, leaving behind a cloud of fire and smoke. These units had a burn time of 2.5 seconds then they were jettisoned. Their thrust was equal to five times the aircraft's gross weight. (Viktor K. Kabanov)

could be raised to an angle of 30 degrees.

The first ZELL take off with a SM-30 was conducted without a pilot because it was determined that there were too many unknown risks to endanger a pilot on the first launch. The first flight proceeded uneventfully over a short, semi-ballistic flight path and the aircraft eventually came back to earth in a crash landing just as planned. Post flight analysis of data generated by the flight verified the viability of the ZELL concept, but also gave cause for a re-evaluation of the launch rail and the construction of its transport assembly. The latter, it turned out, had been all but destroyed during the short time it was exposed to the blast from the PRD-22 rockets and accordingly a major redesign, incorporating an exhaust gas diverter, was undertaken.

Some additional test launchings without pilots followed and revealed (according the test instrumentation) that the G forces on the SM-30 did not exceed 5 Gs. As a result, Georgij Shiyanov and Sergei Anochin, two very experienced pilots from the LII were chosen to conduct the next series of flights.

The PU-30 launcher had been placed on a runway at Zhukovsky, in order to ensure the safe return of the aircraft after a successful launch. In case of trouble, the runway and rescue equipment were quite near. It was determined that the greatest danger actually was from a potential propulsion system failure during the first three to five seconds following launch, as the emergency egress time and altitude were extremely limited.

An initial launch attempt was scrubbed following a booster ignition failure, but three days later on 13 April 1957, Georgij Shiyanov made the first successful test launch. The launch procedure called for the PU-30's launching rail to be raised to 30 degrees and secured by a holdback. The pilot would then start the two AM-5B power plants. When at full power, the afterburners would be started and seconds later the two PRD-22 RATO units would be ignited, which broke the holdback, allowing the aircraft to be launched.

A further four SM-30 launches were successfully accomplished by Georgij Shiyanov and a sixth launch was made by Sergei Anochin. On the seventh flight, 3 June 1957, with Anochin at the controls, the SM-30 carried two 200 gallon drop tanks under the wings. One more test flight was made by Georgij Shiyanov from Zhukovsky before the entire system had been transferred to the NII-VVS (*Nauchno-Issledovatel'skij Institut* or Scientific Research Institute of the Soviet Air Force) in the Astrochan area.

The NII-VVS was responsible to investigate the ZELL method under the rough field conditions. The first NII-VVS pilot to fly the SM-30 was V.G. Ivanov, who successfully accomplished six ZELL launches. Five more NII-VVS pilots each made a successful launch with the SM-30; L.M. Kuvshinov, V.S. Kotlov, M.S. Tvelenyev, A.S. Blagoveshtshenskij and G.T. Beregovoij. After the end of the military test trials a demonstration of the SM-30 was given to the Minister of Defense, Marshall G.K. Jukov. The SM-30 showed its ZELL ability and its outstanding rate of climb, reaching 32,800 feet (10,000 m) within 66 seconds after launch.

One problem which had not been fully solved was the question where the SM-30 should land after accomplishing the mission. The specification issued by the Soviet Air Force asked for a landing run not longer than 1,312 feet (400 m). One solution was that the recovery airfield should be equipped with its own braking system in the form of a line stretched across the runway with parachutes hooked to its ends. The returning SM-30 was expected to hook the line with its landing gear, the canopies of the parachutes filled with air and the aircraft decelerated.

Another solution tested was the installation of a permanently mounted tail hook on the underside of the SM-30, which was lowered on approach to catch an arresting wire strong across the runway. Trials of both systems proved the advantages of the arresting gear system.

The tests with the SM-30 showed that ZELL take off and landing problems had been mastered and the evaluation by the Soviet Air Force revealed that the system was practical under front-line operational condition, but neither the ZELL technology nor the systems for reducing the landing roll of high performance aircraft were pursued.

ZELL Project

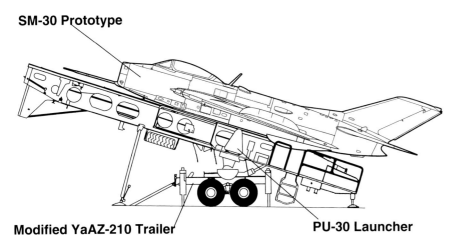

11

MiG-19S Farmer C

SM 9/2 and SM 9/3 Prototypes

Shortly after production of the MiG-19 Farmer A had been launched during early 1954, it became clear that the number of shortcomings in the initial production version would make it necessary to undertake a major redesign of the type. The Farmer A had been placed into mass production in order to supply the regiments of the Soviet Air Forces and the Air Defense with a supersonic fighter regardless a number of serious shortcomings the aircraft had.

The most serious shortcoming of the Farmer A was the lack of adequate control surface effectiveness at supersonic speeds. This caused by the fact that at critical Mach number the effective control surface area was reduced because of shock wave immersion.

A number of studies were conducted by both the MiG Design Bureau and the Central Aero and Hydrodynamics Institute and finally the Soviets decided that a design feature found on its American opponent, the North American F-100 Super Sabre as the best solution;. The Sabre used a slab-type, all moving horizontal stabilator and this type of stabilator was found to eliminate the stability problem with the Farmer.

Work on the improved version begun during early 1954. The SM-9/2 testbed was modified and a third prototype, the SM-9/3 was built. In contrast to the SM-9/2 which was originally rebuilt from the SM-2/2 prototype, the SM 9/3 was an entirely new prototype.

There were a number of external differences between the SM-9/3 and the standard production MiG-19 Farmer A. The small antenna near the nose wheel door was repositioned to the lower fuselage centerline behind the nose wheel bay. The canopy framing was also recontoured and the radio antenna mast on starboard side was reposition more forward than on the standard production Farmer A.

Armament of the SM-9/3 remained the same as on the Farmer A, two NR-23 cannons in the wing roots and an NR-37D cannon in the starboard side of the nose. The aircraft differed from the Farmer A in that it had a gun blast panel fitted on both sides of the fuselage in front of the guns, below the canopy.

An improved control system with a BU-14MS ram and an ARU-2A load adjuster gave the pilot an artificial feel and stick inputs. The installation of this system made the introduction of a dorsal spine necessary to cover the control line runs. This dorsal spine became a feature for

The SM-9/3 prototype on the ramp at the Zhukovsky Test Center during the factory trials held in the Autumn of 1955 while the aircraft was still fitted with a large Farmer A type rudder. The SM-9/3 flew for the first time on 27 November 1955 with Konstantin K. Kokkinaki at the controls. (Wolfgang Tamme)

The SM-9/3 prototype was later modified with a small rudder. The SM-9/3 had the same NR-23 23MM cannon armament as the Farmer A, but carried a gun blast panel on the fuselage in front of the gun which became a standard feature on the early production MiG-19S Farmer Cs. (Yefim Gordon)

the SM-9/3 and the subsequent production versions. In addition, an APS-4 electromechanical backup in the event of total hydraulic system failure was introduced. Another external change was the introduction of a small antenna on top of the rear fuselage.

The entire tail section was completely redesigned due to the change from a conventional elevator type stabilator to the slab type, all moving horizontal stabilator. This single piece stabilator provided pitch control only and had a balance weight added on the fin tip. The Farmer A had two side-by-side air inlets at the base of the stabilator, while the SM-9/3 and the subsequent MiG-19S had a single inlet. The SM 9/3 also had a large blister at the base of the stabilator.

The SOD-57 transponder on starboard side of the stabilator on the Farmer A was deleted and the fin extension was enlarged on the SM-9/3. The starboard inlet on the fin extension was repositioned further back and the conical rear covering of the Syrena 2 tail warning receiver on the stabilizer was enlarged.

In its original configuration, the SM-9/3 prototype carried the same rudder as the Farmer A, but during the factory test trials the rudder was reduced in size. The reduced rudder was also adopted by all standard MiG-19S production versions. Initially, the SM-9/3 had the national markings painted on the rear fuselage, but this was deleted during a later stage of testing.

The SM-9/3 had a third air brake under the fuselage in order to offset the pitching movement caused by the other two air brakes located in the rear half of the fuselage. This measure was necessary since the Farmer A tended to pitch up rather violently, since a low pressure area formed behind the air brakes set up a disturbed air flow pattern under the stabilizers. The Farmer A carried a single air inlet on the tail in front of the engine exhaust, which was deleted on the SM-9/3.

The SM-9/2 arrived at Shukovsky in September of 1954 and flew for the first time on 16 September 1954 with Gregorij A. Sedov at the controls. The factory test trial envelope was flown by Sedov and Georgij K. Mossolov, Konstantin K. Kokkinaki and Vladimit A. Nefyodov. During these trials with the SM-9/2 Georgij Mossolov attained Mach 1.462 at an altitude of 30,500 feet (9,300 m).

A formation of Bulgarian MiG-19S Farmer Cs on approach to their home base near the capital of Sofia during national celebrations on 9 September 1969. These are all early production Farmer Cs with the small gun blast panel. (Jordan Andreev via Mara Chetnev)

The SM-9/2 was followed the SM-9/3, which left the MiG Experimental Shop for Zhukovsky on 26 August 1955 and flew for the first time on 27 November with Konstantin K. Kokkinaki at the controls. Apart from a few details, the SM 9/3 was externally very similar to an early production MiG-19S.

Both aircraft were used for factory test trials and later transferred to the Flight Research Institute. The tests revealed that the flight characteristics and handling of the type were remarkable improved, while its performance was nearly identical to the Farmer A, especially in top speed and rate of climb. After successful State Acceptance the type was evaluated by the Scientific Research Institute of the Soviet Air Force under operational front-line conditions.

MiG-19S Farmer C

Shortly after the Ministry for Aircraft Production cleared the type for production, the first production examples of the MiG-19S followed the Farmer A on the production lines at GAZ-21 and GAZ-153. The latter built the original Farmer A until June of 1956 and for a time in parallel with the MiG-19S. The production of the Farmer A was progressively phased out, not an uncommon situation in the Soviet aviation industry. The designation for the MiG-19S given by the Ministry of Aircraft Production was "Type 26."

There were a number of differences between the SM-9/3 prototype and the first production MiG-19S aircraft built at the two State Aircraft Factories.

The SRD-1M range finder had been relocated from the nose to a position above the port nose wheel door. The round access panel on port side of the air intake was enlarged. On later production batches, the SRD-1M range finder was replaced by the SRD-3 "Grad" range finder. The AKS-3M gun camera remained on the same position, although later production batches were equipped with the AKS-5 gun camera.

Usually a 200 gallon (760 l) drop tank was carried on the BD-3-56 wing pylon, but this pylon could also carry bombs up to 551 pounds (250 kg). A removable pylon behind the main wheel doors could carry an ORO-57K pod with each eight S-5 unguided rockets.

The gun armament was changed with the two wing root NR-23 23MM cannons being replaced by NR-30 30MM cannon and the single NR-37D 37MM cannon was also replaced by an NR-30. Each NR-30 had an ammunition supply of 70 rounds and a rate of fire of 900 rounds per minute. For its time, the NR-30 was a technologically sophisticated weapon which had entered the Soviet Air Force inventory during 1954 The first production versions were equipped with the ASP-5 gunsight, which was replaced by the ASP-5M. Late production variants were upgraded further with the ASP-5N-V3 gunsight.

Avionics installed in the MiG-19S included a RSIU-3M radio, an RV-2 "Kristall" radio altimeter, an ARK-5 "Amur" radio-compass and the SRO-1 "Barii-M" IFF transponder. Late production aircraft were equipped with the SRO-2 IFF system.

The production MiG-19S was equipped with two 7,165 lbst RD-9B single shaft turbojet engines. These engines weighed 1,532 pounds, had a length of seventeen feet six inches and a diameter of two feet two inches. The RD-9 had been developed by the Tushino Machine-Building Design Bureau "Soyuz" in Moscow by a team headed by Aleksandr Mikulin.

Fuel was contained in two rubberized-fabric fuel tanks located in the wing center section and two additional smaller aluminum fuselage tanks with one mounted under each engine exhaust pipe. Total fuel capacity was 573 gallons. Due to high fuel consumption, the aircraft usually carried two 200 gallon (760 l) underwing fuel tanks on most missions. In this configuration the aircraft's top speed was reduced from 902 mph (1,452 kmh) to 714.5 mph (1,150 kmh). Range, in turn, was increased from 863 miles (1,390 km) to 1,367 miles (2,200 km) through the use of these tanks.

During its production life, the MiG-19S was progressively upgraded in avionics, armament and other details. Early production aircraft were equipped with flush type NR-30 cannons, while later aircraft were equipped with NR-30s with gun gas defectors fitted to the cannon muzzle. Early production versions had a small gun blast panel, but the majority of the production run was fitted with a large oval gun blast panel. Later, it was determined that two small square vents, one at the top and another at the bottom of the cannon muzzle would be sufficient to lessen recoil and the large gun blast panel was removed during the aircraft's next general overhaul. In most cases the area where the gun blast panel had been located was slightly darker than the rest of the aluminum fuselage skinning.

Fuselage Development

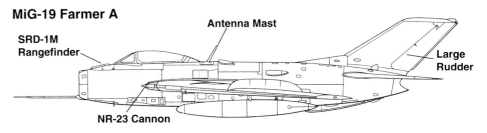

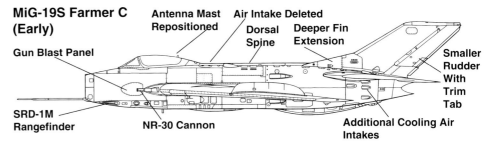

13

A Bulgarian MiG-19S Farmer C of the 19th Fighter Regiment on the ramp at Graf Ignatievo Air Base. The pattern of the taxiway is typical for Eastern Bloc airfields. The repositioned antenna mast, visible beside the canopy identifies this MiG-19 as a Farmer C version. The last Farmer Cs were withdrawn from Bulgarian service during 1978. (Wojciech Luezak).

The fin leading edge extension was also enlarged on late production versions. The starboard side of the enlarged extension had two air intakes instead of the single intake located on the short extension. The original fin extension straddled the dorsal spine making it appear as if the spine came out of the fin extension while the longer fin extension ended on top of the dorsal spine.

Once the MiG-19S had entered service and had been spotted by Western observers, NATO gave the aircraft the ASCC Reporting Name Farmer C. One of the first units outside the Soviet Union to be re-equipped with the MiG-19s was the 24th Air Army which was occupying airfields in the German Democratic Republic (East Germany). On 10 March 1964, a Douglas RB-66C reconnaissance aircraft of the 19th Tactical Reconnaissance Squadron took off from its French Base at Toul for a training mission over West Germany. Allied Air Defense Radar stations sent out several messages for the aircraft to reverse course, but the RB-66 entered East German airspace at 1501 local time. A 24th Air Army MiG-19S was directed by a ground controller to the RB-66 and after firing several warning shots, the Soviet pilot shot the American plane down over Gardelegen. The crew, CAPT David I. Holland (pilot), CAPT Melvin J. Kessler (instructor/navigator) and LT Harold W. Welch (navigator) successfully bailed out and were taken prisoner by the East Germans. They were subsequently handled over to Soviet authorities in Germany. The incident was considered to be serious by the White House and that same day President Johnson personally discussed the situation with Secretary of State Dean Rusk and the his special assistant for national security affairs, McGeorge Bundy. After some negotiations with Soviet authorities, the crew of the RB-66 were released.

Early production MiG-19S Farmer Cs were armed with NR-30 30MM cannon that carried no gun gas deflector (muzzle brake) and had a small gun blast panel on the fuselage side. The tactical number, Blue 30, had a thin Black outline and was rather weathered. (Yefim Gordon)

More than seventy-five percent of the 2,500 Farmers built in the two State Aircraft Factories were MiG-19S variants. Production ended in late 1957, somewhat earlier than had been originally scheduled by the Ministry of Aircraft Production. This was due to the fact that the MiG-21 Fishbed had become available and certain technical shortcomings with the Farmer's engines, airframe and flight characteristics could never totally be solved satisfactory. For this reason GAZ-21 at Nizhny Novgorod was switched to MiG-21 production, while GAZ-153 at Novosibirsk switched to production of the Sukhoi Su-9 Fishpot B.

A constant problem of all MiG-19 version was engine overheating, caused by the side-by-side configuration of the two RD-9B engines. A number of aircraft were lost because of in flight engine fires throughout the Farmer's operational life. It was an important rule that pilots not operate the engines at full throttle or in afterburner for periods longer than recommended in the flight manuals. Failure to heed this warning could easily lead to an in flight engine fire. Another problem area was in the hydraulic system. When at full throttle, the hydraulic lines between the oil tanks and the two RD-9B power plants would rub against the fuselage skin. According the operational manuals, it was important to replace these lines every two years, but the chronic shortage of spare parts in Soviet and foreign regiments often prevented these routine maintenance changes. As a result, after a certain number of flight hours, metal fatigue could cause the lines to fail, and the resulting hydraulic fluid leak would cause an explosion and/or fire in the rear fuselage. This type of fire quickly spread and usually led to the loss of the aircraft.

The rear fuselage fuel tank system also caused problems. After an extended period of flight hours, the rubber used to seal the tank would begin to break down and leak. This could lead to

Cannon And Blast Panel Development

MiG-19S Farmer C Early

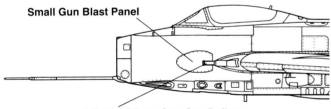

Small Gun Blast Panel

NR-30 Without Gun Gas Deflector

MiG-19S Farmer C Late

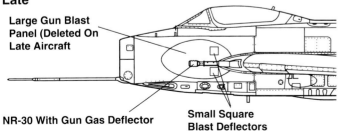

Large Gun Blast Panel (Deleted On Late Aircraft

NR-30 With Gun Gas Deflector

Small Square Blast Deflectors

Two Bulgarian pilots, dressed in VKK-20 pressurized flight suits, pose in front of an early production MiG-19S Farmer C that has a small gun blast panel on the fuselage side. The aircraft has been modified with a late NR-30 cannon with a gun gas deflector (muzzle brake) on the muzzle. (Wojciech Luczak)

fuel collecting in the bottom of the rear fuselage. Ground crews were cautioned to check the rear fuselage prior to flight to make sure there was no pooled fuel. If this was not checked and fuel did pool in this area, an in flight explosion could occur if the aircraft was operated in afterburner for an extended period. This shortcoming was usually solved by replacing the tanks with items made in local maintenance depots. The foreign customers also installed

Late in their operational careers, Bulgarian MiG-19S Farmer Cs received a tactical camouflage with the early two digit Black tactical number being replaced by a three digit White number. This particular MiG-19S, White 882, on the ramp at Graf Ignatievo Air Base carries no national insignia because it is being sold to a Western buyer. (Wojciech Luezak)

This East German MiG-19S, Red 495 (Serial Number 1225), crashed on 7 February 1968 due to an engine fire, a common problem on early MiG-19s. The wing leading edge weapons pylon was only used on the East German MiG-19S Farmer Cs and was a modification done to East German aircraft during regular overhauls (Hans-Joachim Mau)

East German Leading Edge Wing Pylon

MiG-19S Farmer C

East German MiG-19S Farmer C

modified tanks to solve the problem.

The starting procedure for the MiG-19 was demanding. It was necessary to check wind direction before engine start to determine which engine to start first. If the wind came from the port side, the starboard engine had to be started first, when the wind came from the starboard side, the port RD-9B had to be started first, otherwise the other engine could not be started because of insufficient airflow through the single air intake for two engines. An unofficial starting procedure was also introduced by some Soviet regiments and this was quickly adopted by other Warsaw Pact units equipped with the aircraft. According to many ground crewmen, it was the best method to start the RD-9B engines. The fuel pumps were started until a pool of fuel engine was formed on the rear engine combustion chamber, then the starter motor for the turbine was started, providing airflow to the engine. Then a ground crewman would throw a burning rag into the engine exhaust. The RD-9B would start in most of the cases.

Although withdrawn from front-line service, the MiG-19S as well some MiG-19PM served well into the early 1970s. In 1970 there were still 350 examples in the inventory of the Air Defense and Frontal Aviation Regiments of the Soviet Air Force.

The MiG-19S was also exported in various counties. All new production aircraft exported outside the Soviet Union were all built at the GAZ-21 plant at Nizhny Novgorod. Additionally, a large number of ex-Soviet Air Force MiG-19s were exported as the MiG-21 begun to re-equip front-line Regiments. Only three members of the Warsaw Pact received the Farmer C; Bulgaria, Czechoslovakia and the German Democratic Republic.

In July of 1957, the first group of Bulgarian, Czech, Polish and Rumanian pilots and technicians arrived at the training center of Sevastleika near Nizhny Novgorod. These were the first foreigners to receive transition training on the MiG-19S and MiG-19P. Following a theoretical preparation in ground school, pilots underwent flight evaluations in the MiG-15UTI and MiG-17F. After successfully completing this course they began transition training on the MiG-19S during early August.

The first foreign country to be equipped with the MiG-19S was Bulgaria which received twenty-four early production Farmer Cs during 1957. These aircraft had the small gun blast panel and short fin extension. Bulgaria was the only Warsaw Pact country to be equipped with the early version of the MiG-19S. In 1958, a squadron of the 19th Fighter Regiment, based at Graf Ignatievo, was equipped with the MiG-19S. This squadron continued to fly the MiG-19S until 1965 when it struck off charge its last Farmer C. One regiment based at Gabrovnitza was equipped with the MiG-19S between 1958 and 1963. The Regiment was disbanded during 1963 and the aircraft were reassigned to regiments at Uzundjovo and Dobroslavtzi. A single squadron of the Uzundiovo based regiment retained the Farmer C until 1978, when the aircraft were finally struck of charge.

Initially, Bulgarian Farmers carried two digit Black tactical numbers and the national markings on the wing undersurface, the rear fuselage and stabilizer. Late in their operational careers these aircraft were given a camouflage finish and three digit White tactical numbers.

The first twelve MiG-19s Farmer Cs were delivered disassembled to Kbley Air Base in Czechoslovakia in December of 1957. After assembly and flight testing the first aircraft, Black 0859, was turned over to the Czech Air Force on 3 January 1958. On 9 May of that

An East German Air Force MiG-19S, Red 761, on the ramp at Preschen Air Base with an German-built VEB Sachsenring S-4000 truck. This particular MiG-19S was retired from service during May of 1969. The aircraft has been modified with a wing leading edge weapons pylon. (Wolfgang Tamme)

An East German Farmer pilot prepares for a mission from Dresden Airfield during the *Quartett* (Quartet) exercise held in the southern part of the German Democratic Republic between 9 and 14 September 1963. The blister in the bend of the fin extension was a German modification done during regular overhauls. (Wolfgang Tamme)

same year, during a large military parade in Prague, the Farmer Cs were publicly shown for the first time. These aircraft were assigned to the 1st Fighter Regiment at Ceske Budejovice and to the 11th Fighter Regiment at Zatec, both part of the 3rd Air Defense Division. From 1959 on these units also received the license built Farmer C (S-105s) from Czech production.

All Czech MiG-19S carried a Blue outlined national insignia on the top and bottom of the wing and on the fin. Tactical numbers, four digit Black numbers, were applied to the rear fuselage just behind the wing.

On 5 September 1958, the German Democratic Republic (East Germany) signed a contract with the Soviet Union for the delivery of twelve MiG-19S fighters at a price of 15.57 Million Marks. Initially it was planned to convert two *Geschwader* (Regiments) to the Farmer; *Fliegergeschwader 3 "Wladimir Komarow"* and *Fliegergeschwader 8 "Hermann Matern"*, both were, at that time, based at Preschen. The two units were, however, under different parent commands. *Fliegergeschwader 3* was part of the *1. Fliegerdivision* (1st Aviation Division) at Cottbus, while *Fliegergeschwader 8* belonged to the *3rd Fliegerdivision* at Drewitz.

In June of 1959 the first twelve East German pilots departed for Savaslaika Air Base in the Soviet Union for conversion training, which lasted until September of 1959. Ground crews were trained on the same base between March and early September 1959. The first MiG-19S fighters were assigned to the *2. Staffel* (2nd Squadron) of *Fliegergeschwader 3*, which became operational during October of 1959.

The existence of the supersonic MiG-19 was a well guarded secret of the East German Air Force and base security measures were very strict. Handstands had Red circles painted on them which could not be crossed by personnel not associated with the MiG-19. Also, military personnel with no connection to the MiG-19 had strict orders not to approach the aircraft or even look at the Farmer!

Due to the fact that the MiG-21F-13 became available for Warsaw Pact members sooner than anticipated and that the Farmer C was disliked by pilots and the ground crews, the *Fliegergeschwader 8* was not, as originally planned, equipped with the MiG-19, but instead became the first East German Regiment to be equipped with the MiG-21F-13. The major shortcomings of the MiG-19S in German service was a lack of spare parts in general and for the hydraulic system in particular and the difficult maintenance procedures for the type. When East German ground crews and pilots made proposals on how to correct the shortcomings of the MiG-19, these proposals deliberately suppressed by East German authorities and the Communist Party. The pilots and ground crews were threatened by both authorities that

A ground crewman directs a MiG-19S, Red 287 of *Fliegergeschwader 3 "Wladimir Komarow"* from its parking place on the ramp at Prescher Air Base. The aircraft has a short fin extension while the MiG-19S in the background has the long fin extension. All East German Farmer Cs were ex-Soviet Air Force aircraft. (Hans-Joachim Mau)

severe disciplinary action and party punishment would result if they would not withdraw their reports on the problems with the design of the Farmer!

The *Luftstreitkräfte* had both early and late production MiG-19S versions in its inventory. All East German aircraft were ex-Soviet Air Force, not new production aircraft. The early the short-fin MiG-19S were modified at the *Flugzeugwerke Dresden* with a small blister fairing being added at the bend of the fin extension. This fairing housed an improved ARU-3U radio compass and was only used on East German MiG-19S Farmer Cs.

All twelve MiG-19S Farmer Cs were equipped with a pylon on the wing leading edge to accommodate the ORO-57K rocket pod (eight S-5 rockets). East German Farmer Cs were the only aircraft within the Warsaw Pact which were equipped with this type of pylon configuration, all other countries used the standard small rear mounted pylon. This modification was also done by *Flugzeugwerke Dresden*

Of the twelve Farmer Cs delivered, six were lost in accidents. Another Farmer C, Red 602, was struck of charge after a taxing accident. As a result on 1 September 1963, all remaining MiG-19S Farmer Cs and MiG-19PMs were put into a single Staffel, while the two other Squadrons were re-equipped with the MiG-21F-13.

On occasion of the 5th World Aerobatic Championship held at Magdeburg in August of 1968, two MiG-19S Farmer Cs (Serial 1224) Red 844 and (Serial Number 12416) Red 872, were repainted with a special paint scheme for a planned solo aerobatic demonstration over this East German Airfield at the opening of the championship. During a training flight for the solo demonstration on 9 August, *Hauptmann* (Captain) Sigfried Wodzich, commander of the 1st Squadron/3rd Fighter Regiment crashed in Red 844 and was killed. During another training mission, the second MiG-19S, Red 872, flown by *Hauptmann* Heinz Stammberger crash landed on 18 August at Stendal Air Base due to engine and hydraulic failure There was relatively little damage from the crash landing, however, considerable damage was incurred when the aircraft was dismantled for transport to Preschen. The wreckage of this Farmer C was subsequently taken to Kamenz where it rested for several years before the airframe was broken up. As a result of these two accidents, the demonstration flights were canceled.

The last East German flight of a MiG-19s took place on 25 October 1968 with *Hauptmann* Harald Galfe at the controls. After this flight, the last remaining Farmer Cs were stricken off charge and the units re-equipped with the MiG-21 Fishbed. All East German Farmer Cs carried national markings on top and bottom of the wing and on the fin. Until late 1959, no hammer and circle emblem was carried in the national marking. All aircraft carried a three digit Red tactical numbers which carried no outline.

Fin Extension

MiG-19S Farmer C (Early)

Short Fin Leading Edge Extension

MiG-19S Farmer C (Late)

Long Fin Leading Edge Extension

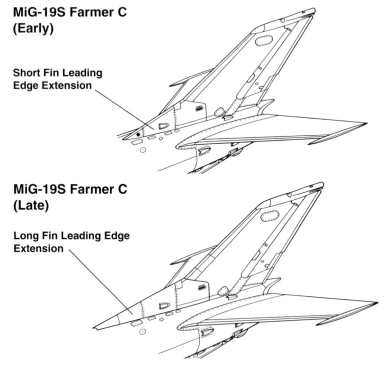

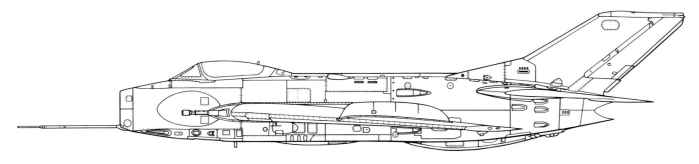

Specification

MiG-19S Farmer C

Wingspan	30 feet 2 inches (9.1 m)
Length	46 feet 11 inches (14.32 m)
Height	12 feet (2.97 m)
Empty Weight	11,402 pounds (5,172 kg)
Maximum Weight	19,096 pounds (8,662 kg)
Power plant	Two 7,165 lbst RD-9B afterburning turbojet engines
Armament	Three NR-30 30ᴍᴍ cannons.
Speed	903 mph (1,453 kph)
Service Ceiling	56,145 feet (17,500 m)
Range	1,243 miles (2,000 km)
Crew	One

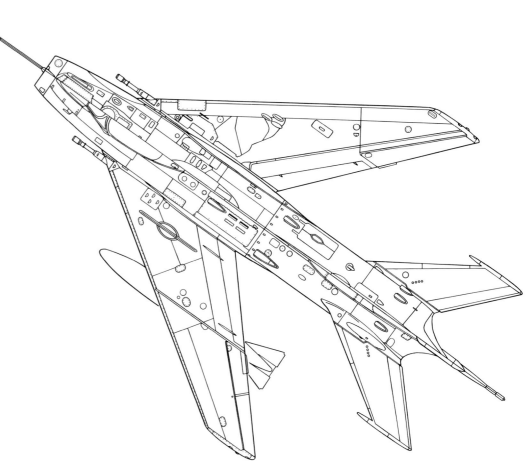

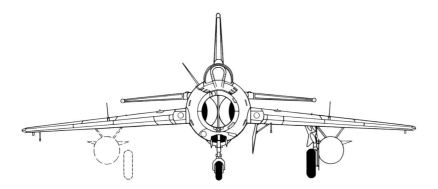

This East German MiG-19S, Red 844 (Serial Number 1224), was later repainted in a special color scheme for the 5th World Aerobatic Championships held at Magdeburg. During training for the event, the aircraft crashed over Magdeburg on 18 August 1968, killing the pilot, *Hauptmann* (Captain) Sigfried Wodzich, commander of the 1st Squadron of the 3rd Fighter Regiment. (Hans-Georg Volprich).

the number of Farmer Cs delivered to Arabic countries thanks to the Israeli Intelligence Agency, the Mossad. During the short but violent Six Day War, Israel claimed twenty-nine MiG-19s from various Arab air forces as destroyed in the air when the conflict ended on 10 June 1967. The IDF/AF claimed a total of 451 Arab aircraft destroyed against forty-five

Red 872 was the second aircraft repainted in the special color scheme for the World Aerobatic Championships. On 18 August 1968, this aircraft crash landed at Stendal Air Base due to an undercarriage failure. The pilot, *Hauptmann* (Captain) Heinz Stammberger was not injured and the wreckage of the aircraft was taken to Kamenz Air Base for examination. (Klaus Meissner)

For ease of maintenance the starboard side NR-30 cannon could be lowered after the fuselage fairing was removed. The large gun blast panel of this East German MiG-19S, Red 844, has been replaced by two square metal sheets bolted to the outside of the fuselage skinning.

The first non-Warsaw Pact country to receive the Farmer C was Egypt, which took delivery of the first aircraft during 1958. A total of 100 Farmer Cs were delivered with the last arriving in June of 1962. These were allocated to six squadrons and had tactical numbers from 3501 to 3599. During the Six Day war with Israel, twenty Egyptian Air Force Farmer Cs were destroyed on the ground on the first day of war (5 June 1967). Eight Farmer Cs that had become airborne that day were shot down by Israeli fighters. To make up these losses, the Soviet Union immediately delivered another sixty Farmer Cs in June of 1967. By early 1985 there were still some sixteen Soviet-built MiG-19s being used as training aircraft within the Egypt air force.

During 1958, Syria received forty MiG-19S Farmer Cs to become the second customer in the Middle East. The West, in particular the United States, had very accurate information on

This Soviet manufactured MiG-19S, Black 1006, was one of two dismantled "pattern aircraft" delivered to the Aero plant at Vodochody to help start license production of the type in Czechoslovakia. It flew on 6 February 1958 as the first Aero assembled MiG-19S. (Zdenek Hurt)

A S-105 (Serial Number 850503) of the fifth and last production batch on the ramp at Vodochody shortly after it rolled off the assembly line during the Summer of 1961. All Czech Farmers had a four digit Black tactical number on the rear half of the fuselage. (Zdenek Hurt)

A Czech ground crew checks a new production S-105 (Serial Number 50302). They have opened the upper access panel for the RD-9B power plant. This aircraft belongs to the third production batch built at Aero and was delivered to the Czech Air Force during 1960. (Zdenek Hurt)

A line-up of new production S-105s on the ramp at the Aero Factory in Vodochody. The fairing above the nose wheel door was the RD-3 "Grad" range finder which was fitted to the port side on the nose in the same position as the NR-30 cannon on the starboard side. (Zdenek Hurt)

admitted losses.

In combat the MiG-19S had proven to be an excellent dog fighter and its three NR-30 cannon gave the Farmer great stopping power against opposing fighters. But, in contrast to the MiG-21 Fishbed and MiG-17 Fresco, it saw only limited air-to-air combat during the war. This was mainly due to the relatively small numbers delivered to the Arab air forces.

In 1960, fifteen Farmer Cs were delivered to the Iraq. Other nations to receive the MiG-19S included fifteen to North Korea and thirty to North Vietnam. The last country to receive the Farmer C was Afghanistan. which received eighteen aircraft during 1965.

Czech Built MiG-19S Farmer C

In 1953 the Supreme Command of the Czech Air Force issued two requirements for a supersonic fighter to be developed and built in Czechoslovakia. The project, coded S-105, called for a daylight fighter with a ceiling 65,000 feet (20,000 m). At this same time they also issued a requirement for a missile equipped all-weather interceptor for altitudes up to 98,000 feet (30,000 m) coded S-200.

It was soon realized by the Aviation Investigation Institute at Lentnany that project S-200 could never be realized with the current capabilities the Czech aviation industry and the project was quietly phased out. On the other hand, however, project S-105 was determined to be possible, especially since an aircraft of a similar category was under development in the Soviet Union. The Czech Ministry of National Defense suggested not to proceed further with

Czech ground crewmen prepare to refuel an overall Natural Metal S-105 (MiG-19S) Farmer C. The rear mounted weapons pylon is visible just above the 200 gallon underwing tank. The interior of the open access panel on this S-105 was painted in a Chromate Green. (Zdenek Hurt)

This S-105, Black 0428 (Serial Number 850428) of the Patrik aerobatic team was painted with a Red nose ring and fin leading edge. The aircraft was from the forth production batch built during 1961. Smoke generators were carried on the underwing pylons for air show performances. (Zdenek Hurt)

A Czech pilot in the cockpit of a Czech-built S-105 Farmer C. The large gun blast panel was replaced by two small square metal panels, although the fuselage skin remains discolored in the shape of the old blast panel. (Zdenek Hurt)

Ground crews perform the final checks on a new production S-105 of the fifth production batch at the ramp at Vodochody during the Summer of 1961. The S-105 was identical to the late production MiG-19S built in the Soviet Union. (Zdenek Hurt)

a nation version of project S-105 and instead to negotiate with the Soviet government for a production license for the MiG-19.

Negotiations between Moscow and Prague subsequently lead to an agreement for license production which was signed in Moscow on 30 July 1956. Under this agreement the MiG-19S would be produced in Czechoslovakia under the designation S-105.

Between 1955 and 1956 technicians from the Aero Vodochody plant traveled to the Soviet Union to learn if it would be possible to switch production at the plant directly from the MiG-15bis to the MiG-19S. Planned Czech Air Force expansion required a production run of approximately 600 aircraft.

In order to allow personnel to get acquainted with the MiG-19S two complete pattern aircraft and thirteen disassembled Farmers (at various stages of completion known as *Rozsypy* aircraft) were shipped from Soviet State Aircraft Factories to the Aero Vodochody factory on the outskirts of Prague. These aircraft were used to allow the Czechs to become familiar with the assembly of the MiG-19S. The first of the two pattern MiG-19S Farmer Cs arrived on 15 May 1957 at Vodochody. Detailed production documentation arrived on 24 August, however, it was discovered that the documentation did not match up with the pattern aircraft or the *Rozsypy* aircraft. This was due to the fact that all the various aircraft came from different production batches and had detail differences between aircraft. Redrawing many of the production drawings resulted in a considerable delay and at one point it was decided to stop all work on the project. Finally, in June of 1958, after months of negotiations with the Soviets, the project was resumed. By the end of 1958, both pattern aircraft and all *Rozsypy* aircraft had been assembled and successfully test flown.

One *Rozsypy* MiG-19S (Serial Number 850012) was converted for the photographic reconnaissance role with the nose mounted NR-30 cannon and a fuselage fuel tank deleted to make room for a AFPN-21B or AFP21KT camera. The type flew for the first time on 25 May 1959, but tests revealed that during low speed flights, the temperature within the camera space was above safe limits for camera and film. Although this problem was solved with the introduc-

Czech-built S-105 (MiG-19S) Farmer Cs on the ramp at the Aero plant in Vodochody awaiting delivery to Czech Air Force fighter regiments. The first digit of the tactical number is a 5 denoting that these aircraft are all part of the fifth production batch. (Zdenek Hurt)

(Right) A line-up of overall Natural Metal Bulgarian Air Force MiG-19S Farmer Cs. All the tactical numbers were in Black and the Bulgarian national insignia was carried on both the rear fuselage and fin. (Attila Bonhardt)

An early production MiG-19S Farmer C, Red 37, of the Soviet Air Force is towed by a GAZ-63 tuck. The air data boom had been retracted to keep it from being damaged while being towed. Oversized tactical numbers, like the ones on this MiG-19, were usually applied to aircraft assigned to training units. (V.I. Pashenko)

The MiG-19SV was designed as a high altitude interceptor. The two NR-30 cannon in the wing root were deleted but the small gun blast panel was retained. Four large air scoops were added to the upper fuselage and an avionics blister was installed on each wing tip. (Yefim Gordon)

The SM-9/3T was designed as a missile armed interceptor equipped with two R-3R infrared homing air-to-air guided missiles (NATO reporting name AA-2 Atoll). For testing the aircraft carried a camera on the lower fuselage just in front of the engine exhausts and the the EKSR-46 flare dispenser on the fin was repositioned. The single SM-9/3T prototype first flew on II February 1959. (Viktor Kulikov)

The SM-9/3T prototype was given the tactical number Blue 08. It was armed with two R-3S (AA-2 Atoll) missiles mounted on APU-26 missile rails. Two recording cameras were fitted under the starboard wing while a single camera was carried under the port wing. The aircraft retained the starboard NR-30 cannon. (Yefim Gordon)

tion of four cooling air inlets, the project was canceled during 1960. Another project that did not proceed beyond the design study phase was a two seat trainer variant of the S-105.

Once MiG-19S production was fully established the *Rozspy* MiG-19S Farmer Cs were returned to the Aero factory for modification and upgrading to current production standards, making them identical to the license built S-105 Farmer Cs.

Production of the first batch of S-105s (S for Stihac of Fighter) started in 1959 and these aircraft contained a number of components supplied by the Soviet Union. The first S-105 (Serial 850101) designated for static testing was transferred to the Research and Test Center at Letnany where trials were conducted between 6 June and 13 October 1959. The second aircraft was rolled out on 17 October 1959 and was selected for the flight testing. It made its first flight on 30 October 1959. By the end of 1959 the four remaining S-105 of the first production batch were completed.

While the first batch was considered to be a pre-series batch with the six S-105s used mainly for testing, the second and third production batches were considered to be serial production batches and all S-105s from these two batches were built and delivered during 1960. All S-105s from the second batch were short fin versions. S-105s of the third and all subsequent production batches were all long fin versions, similar to late production Soviet MiG-19S Farmer Cs. S-105s of the fourth and fifth production batches were all manufactured during 1961. A total of 103 S-105s were produced in five batches by the Aero factory at Vodochody. The last two were delivered on 29 November 1961 and production then shifted to the Aero L-29 two seat trainer.

The Czech built S-105 was identical to the Soviet-built MiG-19S and could be only identified by its four digit Black tactical number on the rear fuselage. The first two digits stood for

The SM-50 was fitted with a RU-013 liquid fuel rocket housed in a U-19 rocket-fuel container under the fuselage. The wing root armament was deleted, but the small gun blast panel was retained. The SRD-1M range finder was relocated to a position in front of the canopy and an antenna has been added to the nose. (O.V. Luzenko)

The SM-50 had the large centerline ventral fin replaced by two smaller side-by-side ventral fins. The EKSR-46 flare dispenser on the fin was deleted and the opening faired over. Additionally, there was no trim tab on the rudder, even though this was a standard fitting on production MiG-19S Farmer Cs. (A.A. Zirnov)

the production batch, the last two digits for the individual aircraft within the production batch. An S-105 with the tactical number Black 0204 was the 4th aircraft of the second production block. With only five production blocks, the first two digits of Czech-built aircraft ranged between 01 and 05.

The production of the S-105 in Czechoslovakia filled the gap between MiG-15bis and the MiG-21F-13 production. Since there was no other project being worked on at the Aero company at Vodochody, production of the MiG-19S assured work for the technicians and skilled workers and provided the Czech aviation industry with vital knowledge on modern manufacturing techniques for supersonic aircraft. This experience was of great help in the production of the MiG-21F-13 and certainly had influence on the Aero L-29 production line. Czechoslovakia was the only country within the Warsaw Pact to build the MiG-19.

After production phased out, the plant was still active conducting overhauls of both Czech and Soviet MiG-19s. The last Farmer C was withdrawn from operational service with the Czech Air Force on 2 July 1972.

MiG-19SV Farmer C

During the cold war, Western reconnaissance aircraft violated Soviet and Warsaw Pact airspace on a regular basis. The most serious threat came from the high altitude English Electric Canberra FR7 and the Martin RB-57D, which deliberately violated Soviet airspace during their intelligence missions.

In December of 1954 Lockheed, the CIA and the USAF began work on the first U-2 reconnaissance aircraft at the Skunk Works in Burbank, California. On 4 July 1956, the first mission over the Soviet Union was flown by an U-2 from Wiesbaden Air Base in West Germany.

When the first information on the altitude capabilities of the U-2 (70,000 feet plus) arrived in the Soviet Union, it was viewed with some alarm. The Soviet Air Force had nothing that could even come close to being capable of intercepting a U-2. This situation led to Project SM-9V (V for *Vysotnij* or altitude) at the MiG Design Bureau. It was given a top priority and the requirement issued in 1955 was to develop, as soon as possible, a fighter able to intercept high flying Western reconnaissance aircraft.

The basic lay-out was adopted from the MiG-19S Farmer C, but the airframe was reduced considerably in overall weight to increase the aircraft's high altitude performance. The two wing root NR-30s cannons were removed leaving only fuselage mounted NR-30 cannon for armament. The SRD-1M range finder was again repositioned, this time from the port side above the nose wheel door to a position in front of the canopy. This was the original configuration of the MiG-19SV, but some models retained the standard armament of three NR-30 cannons and had the SRD-1M range finder in its original position. They could only be identified as MiG-19SVs by the four large air intakes on the rear fuselage.

Other weight reduction measures included removal of the TP-19 drag chute and RV-2 radio altimeter including its antennas on the wing undersurfaces. For flights at extreme altitudes, a KKO-1 oxygen system was installed. The MiG-19SV used a 7,275 lbst RD-9BF engine which required additional cooling air. To meet this requirement, four large cooling air inlets were added to the rear fuselage.

After all weigh saving measures were taken, the MiG-19SV weighed some 507 pounds less than a standard MiG-19S, the overall weight was 12,301 pounds (5,580 kg). In parallel to the SM-9V the Soviet Air Force developed the VSS-04A high altitude pressure suit, which was very uncomfortable and highly restrictive of pilot movement, but it assured the survival of the pilot up to altitudes of 80,000 feet (25,000 m). Although developed for the SM-9V project, the suit was soon issued to Farmer C units since it became clear that the slightest in flight emergencies could quickly affect the integrity of the pressure cockpit and lead to the death of the pilot.

The SM-9V first flew in 1956 and the factory test program was under the leadership of Konstantin K. Kokkinaki and Vladimir A. Nefyodov. The aircraft was produced in small numbers under the designation MiG-19SV and on 6 December 1956 test pilot N.I. Korovochkin from the Scientific Research Institute of the Air Force set a new altitude record of 68,044.6 feet (20,740 m) during operational trials with the type. At approximately this same time the CIA launched the first long endurance flights over the Soviet Union with the U-2. According published CIA figures, about 30 such missions were carried out up to May of 1960,

This MiG-19SV, Red 17, was placed in storage after it finished flight testing. The MiG-19SV had the same armament as the Farmer C and featured small gun blast panels on the fuselage. The aircraft had four large cooling air intakes on the rear fuselage in place of the small intakes normally carried on the Farmer C. (A. A. Zirnov)

when CIA pilot Francis Gary Powers was shot down near Sverdlovsk in the Urals Military District.

Some late production batches of the MiG-19SV were powered by the improved RD-9BF-2 power plant. The MiG-19SV had identical handling characteristics to the MiG-19S, although the top speed was about 18.6 mph (30 km/h) better than the MiG-19S. Despite this improvement, the MiG-19SV could not stop the violations over the Soviet Union. During Operation OVER FLIGHT, as aerial espionage over the Soviet Union was called, the U-2's cameras produced thousands of sharp photographs of Soviet military installations. Moscow protested in secret, since it did not want the world to know that Soviet anti-aircraft weapons and interceptor fighters could not stop the U-2. During these missions CIA pilots watched as MiG-19s and MiG-21s tried in vain to get near them, but fell away as they lacked the necessary high attitude performance.

In parallel with high altitude interceptor fighters, the Lavochkin Design Bureau had developed the V-75 Dvina (known to NATO as the SA-2 Guideline) air defense missile. This was done because the Soviet leadership was more confident in missiles than in interceptor fighters and as a result more research and development money from the defense budget was spent on missiles.

MiG-19R Farmer C

The MiG-19R (R for Razvedchik or Observer) was a reconnaissance version of the MiG-19S which was built in limited numbers. This daylight reconnaissance version carried a set of AFA-39 cameras mounted in a special ventral compartment.

SM-9/3T Farmer C

In 1958, the Soviet Union started to copy the American Philco-Ford AIM-9 Sidewinder air-to-air missile under the designation R-3S (NATO name - AA-2 Atoll). In order to develop a launching carrier for air-to-air launch tests, an early MiG-19S was modified to perform the trails.

The infrared-homing R-3S (Device 310A) had a length of 7.6 feet (2.838 m) and weighs 161.5 pounds (73.3 kg). Its big disadvantage is that it can only be launched from the rear aspect of the target. It has a burn time of 21 seconds and was equipped with an optical proximity fuse. When the warhead was detonated it spread about 1,000 splinters in a circular pattern.

This modified Farmer received the designation SM-9/3T and had the port wing mounted NR-30 cannon and its gun blast panel deleted. On starboard side, the fuselage mounted NR-30 cannon was also deleted, while the wing root mounted NR-30 and its large gun blast panel were retained. It also had only two air intakes on the rear fuselage instead of the four normally found on the MiG-19S. The EKSR-46 flare dispenser on port side of the fin was also slightly repositioned.

During the course of the missile launch trials two cameras were fitted on either side of the APU-26 missile rail which was mounted on the starboard wing. A single camera was also mounted inboard on the port wing to record the launching trials. An additional camera was mounted on the rear fuselage just in front of the engine exhaust.

An APU-26 missile rail was fitted on the standard BD-3-56 wing pylon to accommodate the R-3S. A feature of the APU-26 rail was that the missile could not be launched until the undercarriage was locked in the up position.

The single SM-9/3T, Blue 08, flew for the first time on 11 February 1959 with Aleksandr V. Fedotov at the controls. The factory test program was conducted under A.V. Fedotov and Pyotr M. Ostapenko. The aircraft carried the tactical markings on the nose with a thin Black outline and the national markings were applied on both the top and bottom of the wing. During the trials, R-3S launches were made at Mach 1.245 at an altitude of 35,433 feet (10,800 m). The tests also revealed that the missile launch had no significant influence on the flight characteristic of the SM-9/3T.

SM-50 Farmer C

A number of projects were launched by the MiG Design Bureau in order to develop the fast climbing interceptor into a reliable weapon against Western reconnaissance aircraft which, due to their high altitude capability, fly across the Soviet Union at will.

The SM-50 emerged from the MiG-19S and was also influenced by the SM-30 ZELL trials. The prototype was an early MiG-19S airframe modified with a liquid propellant RU-013 rocket motor mounted under the fuselage.

The gun armament was deleted and the gun ports faired over. The SRD-1M range finder was repositioned from the port side above the nose wheel door to in front of the canopy. The small antenna at the rear of the nose wheel bay was relocated to the port side of the air intake. On fin, the EKSR-46 flare dispenser was deleted and the opening faired over. The large centerline ventral fin was also deleted in favor of two smaller side-by-side ventral fins. The number of cooling air inlets on the rear fuselage was reduced to two and no trim tab was fitted on the rudder.

The SM-50 was equipped with two 7,054 lbst (3,200 kg) RD-9BM engines as well as the under fuselage rocket. The RU-013 rocket motor was housed in a U-19D rocket-plus-fuel unit developed by D.D. Sevruk from the MiG Design Bureau and weighed 745 pounds (338 kg).

The factory flight tests were conducted by Vladimir A. Nefyodov who attained an altitude of 78,740 feet (24,000 m) with the SM-50. The type was able to reach 65.600 feet (20,000 m) in only eight minutes, had a top speed of 1,118 mph (1,800 kmh) and a range of 497 miles (800 km). There were a total of five SM-50 built at GAZ 21.

MiG-19P Farmer B

SM-7/1 and SM-7/2 Prototypes

Shortly after the introduction of the radar equipped MiG-17PF into service with the Soviet Air Defense Command, its commanders realized that the type could not successfully intercept aircraft such as the Royal Air Force Canberra PR III and USAF RB-57D photo-reconnaissance aircraft. These aircraft were making routine penetrations of the airspace east of the Iron Curtain to keep tabs on the Soviet build-up in eastern Europe. In the early 1950s the Soviet Union lacked a weapon which could stop these over flights. Combat reports from Soviet pilots engaged in combat in Korea were also alarming. When the USAF switched to night bombing mission with Boeing B-29 Superfortress heavy bombers, MiG-15s could not be used to intercept them. This experience again showed the immediate need for an all-weather interceptor to equip air defense units.

Top priority was given toward the development of a supersonic, radar equipped all-weather interceptor. Work was performed in parallel with the day fighter SM-9 project and a number of its design features were adopted. The MiG OKB gave the all-weather interceptor project the designation SM-7.

The biggest challenge for the MiG designers was to install the heavy RP-1 Izumrud (Emerald) NATO reporting name, Scan Can, radar sytsem into the nose compartment. The RP-1 (RP, Radio Pricel or Radar Device) consisted of two separate radars. The search radar was used an AR-18-16 antenna mounted on the intake splitter assembly. The conical-scan radar used an AR-18-1 antenna which was mounted on the upper intake lip. Both antennas were driven by AR-18-9 electric motors. The radar system was powered by two GSR-ST-6000A generators.

The first prototype of the radar equipped interceptor was built using the SM-9/1 (the prototype for the Farmer A) under the designation SM-7/1. The nose section was stretched by 14 inches (360MM) and the prototype used radomes that were very similar to those used on the

The SM-7/1 on the runway at Zhukovsky during flight testing which was conducted during 1954. The antenna mast has been moved forward and two 200 gallon (760 liter) drop tanks have been mounted on the underwing pylons. The prototype carried no armament. (Viktor Kulikov)

MiG-17PF.

The prototype left the MiG experimental shop during July of 1954, some seven month after the SM-9/1 and was immediately transferred to Zhukovsky where Vladimir A. Nefyodov made the first flight on 28 August 1954. The factory test trials lasted until 15 December of that same year. During the evaluation program a total of forty-three flights were made by various test pilots. During the tests the SM-7/1 was modified internally, however, the only external modification was that the starboard antenna mast was reposition further to the rear on the fuselage.

The SM-7/1 was followed by the SM-7/2 which differed in a number of details from the first prototype. No armament was initially installed on the SM-7/1, but the SM-7/2-had an armament of two NR-23 cannon installed in the wing roots with a small gun blast panel on each side of the fuselage.

The first prototype had no front airbrake while the SM-7/2 was equipped with this airbrake. An additional air intake and antenna were installed on top of the dorsal spine and the fin extension was enlarged.

While the SM-7/1 had a large rudder and the two piece horizontal stabilizer, the SM-7/2 had control surfaces like the SM-9/3 with a smaller rudder and the single piece slab-type horizontal stabilators with balance weights fitted on the tips.

MiG-19P Farmer B

Production of the radar equipped interceptor started in 1955 at GAZ-21 under the designation MiG-19P. These aircraft were immediately issued to *Istrebitelnaya Aviatsiya* (Interceptor Squadrons) of the PVO (*Protivovozdushnaya Oborona* or Air Defense). All MiG-19Ps and later MiG-19PMs were built at the State Aircraft Factory 21 at Nizhny Novgorod.

The standard production MiG-19P differed in a number of ways from the SM-7/2 prototype. The search radar radome mounted in the intake splitter assembly was much more conical in

The SM-7/1 prototype in its original configuration with the radio antenna mast placed on the rear of the canopy frame. The SM-7/1 had two piece stabilator similar to the early MiG-19 Farmer A. (Viktor Kulikov)

This MiG-19 Farmer A, Blue 26, was assigned to a Frontal Aviation Regiment during mid-1955.

Bulgaria was the first export customer for the MiG-19S Farmer C, receiving thirty aircraft during 1957. Late in their operational careers, Bulgarian Farmers were camouflaged.

This East German Farmer C was one of two painted in this special scheme for the Fifth World Aerobatic Championships. Both aircraft crashed during training and neither flew during the championships.

This MiG-19P Farmer B took part in the Warsaw Pact invasion of Czechoslovakia during the Spring of 1968. All aircraft involved in the operation had two Red recognition stripes painted on the rear fuselage.

The Romanian Air Force operated about forty-five MiG-19PM Farmer Es as part of a mixed air defense regiment. All Romanian MiG-19s used three digit Blue tactical numbers.

This MiG-19PM Farmer E was flown by 31st Fighter Interceptor Regiment of the Hungarian Air Force.

This is an early production Shenyang J-6 Farmer of the Peoples Liberation Army Air Force.

The Egyptian Air Force was equipped with two fighter brigades of late production Shenyang F-6 Farmer Cs, with the bullet shaped braking parachute housing at the base of the fin.

Albania is the only European country to fly the Shenyang F-6. This Farmer was assigned to Regiment 5646 based at Lezha-Zadrima.

Bangladesh operates a number of ex-Pakistani Air Force TF-6 Farmer trainers. This aircraft is assigned to No 25 Squadron at Chittagong Air Base.

The SM-7/1 had an RP-1 Izumurd-1 radar with the antenna under a radome that was very similar to that of the MiG-17PF. This was replaced on the production MiG-19P with a conical radome in the air intake splitter assembly. During trials at Zhukovsky two ORO-57K rocket pods were carried on underwing pylons. (MiG OKB)

Fuselage Development

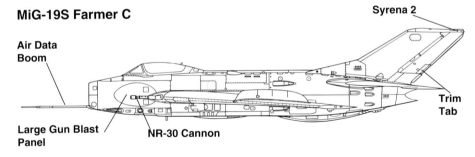

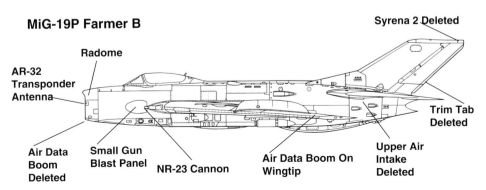

The second prototype was designated the SM-7/2 and differed from from the SM-7/1 in having two NR-23 cannon fitted in the wing roots, with a small gun blast panel added on the fuselage sides in front of the guns. The SM-7/2 was equipped with single piece slab type horizontal stabilators with balance weight on the tips. (MiG OKB)

shape than on the SM-7/2, the radome on the prototype being very similar to that of the MiG-17PF. Several access panels (one square one round) were added on port side of the nose. Most production MiG-19Ps also carried on either side of the nose a small AR-32 button shaped antennae for the SRO-2 transponder system. The canopy framing was altered and a dorsal spine was introduced. As a result, the air inlet on top of the fuselage spine and the aerial on the rear of the fuselage spine were deleted. Four louvers were installed midway on the upper fuselage and on the base of the fin extension two additional air inlets were installed and four cooling air inlets were added in front of the engine exhaust area. The Syrena tail warning radar received on the fin was deleted.

There were also a number of differences between the MiG-19P and MiG-19S Farmer C, the most noticeable being the radar installation. Another major difference was the repositioning of the air-data boom. The MiG-19S had the boom mounted under the air intake, the MiG-19P had the boom relocated to the starboard wing tip. The AKS-3M gun camera fitted on top of the air intake was replaced by a S-13-100-OS gun camera placed in a fairing on the starboard side of the nose.

The oxygen supply for the pilot was increased to five bottles (five liters each) and the radio system was improved. Early variants carried the RSIU-3MG radio, while later MiG-19Ps were equipped with a RSIU-4V radio.

The MiG-19S used an armament of three NR-30 cannons, this was changed on the MiG-19P to two NR-23 23MM cannon with 120 rounds per gun in the wing roots. This was done as a weight saving measure. The large gun blast panel on both sides of the fuselage had been replaced by smaller panels, identical to those used on early versions of the Farmer C. The starboard nose mounted NR-30 was deleted, as was the SRD-1 range finder. The Farmer B was also capable of carrying an ORO-57K rocket pod on a pylon behind the main undercarriage.

The position of the cooling air inlets on the rear fuselage was completely redesigned. The MiG-19S had three inlets vertically in a line, while the MiG-19P only had only two intakes

This MiG-19P, Blue 28, is being used as an instructional aircraft at a ground crew training center. The rear canopy had been completely removed, but the ejection seat has been retained. The aircraft has both 200 gallon (760 liter) fuel tanks on the underwing pylons. (Yefim Gordon)

and these were slightly staggered. Additionally, the front inlet, which was placed right behind the rear air brake on the MiG-19S was repositioned to the rear on the MiG-19P.

While early Farmer B were equipped with the RP-1 radar, the majority of MiG-19Ps were fitted with the improved RP-5 (NATO designation, Scan Odd). The RP-5 had an improved scan pattern and different pulse repetition frequencies for the search and track radars. Externally there was no difference between these two radars systems. The RP-5 Scan Odd worked in conjunction with the optical gunsight ASP-5NM.

Some MiG-19Ps had the SRO-2 transponder aerial moved from the bottom of the fuselage to the port nose behind a round access hatch. As a field modification, some MiG-19Ps were equipped with a MiG-19PM type rudder, which included a trim tab. In its original configuration, the Farmer B rudder had no trim tab.

The MiG-19P became the first supersonic all-weather interceptor to enter service in the Soviet Union and these aircraft were based in sensitive areas within the country that were targets of Western over flights. Soviet PVO pilots made numerous attempts to shoot down these intruders, but without success. The MiG-19Ps were able to shot down the balloons that were equipped with automatic cameras, which were launched in Western Europe. On 9 April 1960, an Western spy plane intruded the Soviet Union in the South, but the MiG-19Ps were unable to intercept it. On 1 May, International Labor Day, the Farmer B was also involved in the shooting down of a CIA U-2 (Article 360). Francis Gary Powers took off from Peshawar Air Base in Pakistan for a 3,700 mile flight across the Soviet Union to the Norwegian air base at Bodo. The Pentagon and the State Department expected to be able to photograph important sites, such as industrial centers, strategic bomber airfields and anti-aircraft missile positions along the route.

South of Sverdlovsk the first V-750 Dvina (SA-2) missiles were launched, but none of them hit the U-2. There was a Sukhoi Su-9 at Sverdlovsk Air Base, which was on a ferry flight from a workshop to a PVO Regiment. The aircraft carried no armament and the pilot, CAPT I. Mientyukov did not have a pressure suit. Nevertheless he was ordered to intercept the U-2

This overall Natural Metal Soviet Air Defense Forces (PVO) MiG-19P Farmer B, tactical number Blue 22, is unusual in that it carries Soviet national markings on the wing upper-surface. (A.A. Zirnov)

and to destroy the target by ramming it. CAPT Mientyukov was directed by a ground controller against the U-2 but was unable to locate the intruder. Due to extensive use of the afterburner, the fuel tanks were soon empty and the Su-9 had to return to the base.

At 0843 local time, two MiG-19Ps, flown by CAPT B. Ayvazyan and LT S. Safronov took off from Sverdlovsk to intercept Power's U-2. After a few minutes, they noticed a huge explosion, which they believed to be a V-75 self-destruct, but in fact it was the U-2, which

Pilots scramble to man their MiG-19Ps on the ramp of a Soviet Air Force base. The tactical numbers on these MiG-19P Farmer Bs indicate that the aircraft are allocated to a training regiment. Tactical numbers in the higher ranges (such as these in the 60s) were usually allocated to training aircraft. (Yefim Gordon)

Polish ground support crewmen and an armament crew poses among with Soviet officers in front of a Soviet Air Force MiG-19P on an improvised airstrip in Czechoslovakia. These forces deployed to Czechoslovakia during the Warsaw Pact invasion of September 1968. (Wojciech Luczak)

The first Polish MiG-19P Farmer Bs were assigned to the 28th Fighter Regiment during mid-1958. Ground crewmen prepare Red 724 for another mission. It was not unusual to find spare parts and other equipment, such as the tow bar and spare tire in the foreground, cluttering the ramps on Warsaw Pact bases. (Zolnierz Polski via Andrzei Morgala)

Polish ground crewmen assist a Soviet pilot in the cockpit of his MiG-19P during the Warsaw Pact invasion of Czechoslovakia in September of 1968. The aircraft carries two Red identification stripes around the rear fuselage. These stripes were carried by all Warsaw Pact aircraft involved in the campaign. (Wojciech Luczak)

Polish ground crews uncover the cockpit of a MiG-19P Farmer B, Red 724, of the 28th Fighter Regiment at Slupsk prior to a mission. The tactical number is repeated in White on the Red air intake cover. The blister on the starboard side of the air intake is the gun camera housing. (Zoinierz Polski via Andrzej Morgala)

Ground crewmen recover the TP-19 drag chute of a Polish MiG-19P Farmer B. The fin tip was painted Red, denoting that the aircraft was assigned to the first squadron of the 28th Fighter Regiment. (Zolnierz Polski via Andrzei Morgala)

was hit by one of the SA-2s. According Soviet reports, a total of fourteen missiles were fired at the U-2.

Since it was unclear to the commander of the military district that the U-2 had been destroyed, the two MiG-19Ps were ordered to continue their search for the target and a new salvo of SA-2s was fired. The missiles would self-destruct when they found no target and the debris jammed the radars of the two MiG-19Ps. Additionally, LT S. Safronov's aircraft was hit by one of the missiles and he was forced to eject. He did not survive the decent and CAPT Ayvazyan was forced to dive his aircraft to avoid another missile. This was the last U-2 over flight of the Soviet Union.

When the R-3S (AA-2 Atoll) air-to-air missile became available in quaintly, a number of MiG-19Ps were converted to act as R-3S missile carriers. The aircraft were modified with a pylon and missile rail under each wing. One drawback was that the MiG-19P could only carry the infrared variant of the R-3S, since the RP-5 radar was not compatible with the R-3R (AA-2 Advanced Atoll) with semi-active radio guided missile. For training missions, the R-3U and R-3P dummy missiles could be carried. These contained the necessary electronics needed for training but did not carry either a rocket motor or explosive warhead. The R-3S modification was introduced as a field modification kit and no aircraft were modified on the production line. The kits were also issued to countries outside the Soviet Union which flew the MiG-19P, such as Bulgaria.

When the more advanced MiG-19PM and MiG-21F-13 became available to the Air Defense regiments, a number of MiG-19Ps were allocated to Frontal Aviation Regiments or training units. A number of these surplus Farmer Bs were also exported.

During the Czech campaign in the Autumn of 1968, the Soviets rushed every fighter available from the Carpathian Military District into action, including a number of obsolete MiG-19Ps. These aircraft were painted with two Red identification bands around the rear fuselage. This special marking was carried by all Soviet fighters involved in the Czech invasion. The first MiG-19Ps arrived in Czechoslovakia during September of 19, however, due to a lack of Soviet ground crews, the MiG-19Ps were serviced by Polish ground crews.

PVO MiG-19Ps all carried two digit Blue tactical numbers, most with a thin Black outline. This color was used exclusively by units assigned to air defense duties.

The MiG-19P was delivered to four Warsaw Pact nations; Bulgaria, Czechoslovakia, Poland and Rumania. Most of these aircraft had seen pervious service in PVO Regiments before being exported.

A ground crewman assists the pilot of this Romanian MiG-19P Farmer B from the cockpit after a mission. Romanian pilots reportedly were generally not satisfied with the flying characteristics of the MiG-19P and the aircraft did not have a long career in the Romanian Air Force. (Dan Antoniu)

A MiG-19P Farmer B, Red 310, of the Romanian Air Force. A distinctive feature of Romanian Farmer Bs was the painting of the upper wing root in Black. There were only a limited number of Farmer Bs taken into the inventory of the Romanian Air Force and most were fitted with 200 gallon (760 liter) drop tanks as standard equipment. (Dan Artoniu)

This Romanian Air Force MiG-19P Farmer B carries two ORO-57K rocket pods on the underwing pylons. The antenna on the port side of the nose is an SRO-2 transponder aerial. Its position is unusual in that most Farmer Bs carried the aerial behind the nose wheel bay. The pilot is equipped with a Second World War style leather flying helmet rather that a crash helmet usually seen on jet fighter pilots. The two guns are NR-23 23MM cannons, standard armament for the MiG-19P. (Dan Antoniu)

(Above and Below) The fuselage skin of this Romanian MiG-19P, Red 802, was removed on the port side and the wings and horizontal stabilizer were removed in order to reveal its internal structure. Retired front-line combat aircraft were often prepared in this manner and displayed in technical universities or officer schools within the Warsaw Pact. (Dan Antoniu)

During the second half of 1957, twenty-seven crated MiG-19Ps were delivered to Kbely Air Base. After reassembly the aircraft were handed over to the Czech Air Force. These aircraft were assigned to the same units flying the MiG-19S in the 1st Fighter Regiment at Ceske Budejovice and the 11th Fighter Regiment at Zatec.

In mid-1958 the first MiG-19Ps were delivered to one Eskadra (Squadron) of the 28th Pulk Lotnictwa Mysliwskiego (28th Fighter Regiment) "Koszalin" based at Slupsk-Redzikowo. The introduction of the Farmer B into Polish service was hampered since all the technical documentation and servicing instructions delivered to Poland were for the MiG-19S Farmer C, not the MiG-19P. The Polish MiG-l9Ps were shown for the first time to the public during an Air Parade on 22 July 1959. When Poland re-equipped with the MiG-21PFM during 1966, most of their remaining MiG-19Ps were transferred to Bulgaria. All Polish MiG-19Ps carried three digit unoutlined Red tactical numbers and the national markings were applied to the rear fuselage, tail fin and wing undersurfaces, but not on the upper wing surface.

In 1959 a total of ten MiG-19Ps were delivered to Rumania, followed a year later by additional five MiG-19Ps. Like Poland, Rumania had not flown the Farmer C and most Romanian pilots were not impressed with the flying characteristics of the type. Only the Divizia 66 Aviatie Vinatoare (66th Fighter Regiment) at Deveselul was equipped with MiG-19Ps and MiG-19PMs. Later the unit moved to Boreca Air Force Base. Initially, tactical numbers Red 001 to Red 015 were assigned to the MiG-19Ps, although in 1965 the first digit of the tactical number was changed from 0 to 7. Shortly before the end of its operational service the first digit of the tactical number was again changed from 7 to 8. National markings were applied to the rear fuselage, tail fin and wing undersurface, but not on the wing uppersurfaces. Romanian MiG-19Ps and later MiG-19PMs had part of the upper wing root painted in Black. The primary duty of the Farmer unit was air defense of Bucharest, the Romanian capital. Some Romanian MiG-19Ps carried the SRO-2 transponder aerial on the port side of the nose, fitted on a round access hatch. Romanian Farmer Bs were also armed with the ORO-57K rocket pod.

The Bulgarian Air Force operated one squadron of MiG-19Ps as part of the air defense regiment at Dobroslavtzi. The first examples arrived in 1966 and were all ex Polish aircraft, having served with the 28th and 39th Fighter Regiments. Bulgarian MiG-19Ps all carried three digit unoutlined Red tactical numbers. The last Bulgarian MiG-19Ps were retired from service during 1975.

MiG-19PG Farmer B

The MiG-19PG differed from the standard MiG-19P Farmer B in having Gorizont-1 equipment installed. This equipment allowed the fighter to be guided to its target by a ground control intercept system. Externally, the aircraft could be identified by an antenna on the port side for the Gorizont-1 system. Additionally, the conical covering for the search radar, mounted in the intake splitter assembly was lengthened and the aircraft had no SRO-2 transponder antennas on the nose. The testbed also lack of the cooling air inlets on the rear fuselage.

This MiG-19P Farmer B, Red 15, was assigned to one of the technical schools of the Soviet Air Force after being withdrawn from front-line service. The aircraft was used an an instructional aircraft for ground crew trainees. (V.I. Pashenko)

Ground crews perform avionics checks on a MiG-19P Farmer B, Red 63, on the ramp of a Soviet training base. Such high tactical numbers were usually allocated to training units. The tactical number on this Farmer B, Red 63, is also oversized, a common practice for aircraft assigned to training units. (V.I. Pashenko)

MiG-19PM Farmer E

In the mid-1950s the first radio guided Soviet air-to-air missile, the RS-2U (AA-1 Alkali) became available for service use. It was first used operationally on the MiG-17PM Fresco E, which became the Soviet Union's first all-weather missile armed fighter.

On 7 January 1956, project SM-7/M was launched with the aim of convert the standard cannon armed MiG-19P to carry and launch the RS-2U missile. Since a number of vital components, such as the RP-2U radar and the APU-4 launching rails could easily be adopted from the MiG-17PM, conversion work progressed quickly and in late January of 1956 the SM-7/M was taken to Zhukovsky for factory flight testing.

The type quickly cleared both factory and state trials and series production of the type started at GAZ 21 under the designation MiG-19PM that same year.

The RS-2U (NATO reporting name AA-1 Alkali) was a beam riding air-to-air missile which consisted of a fuse and warhead (first section), steering fins and autopilot (second section), rocket engine and batteries (third section), stabilizing fins and pneumatic system (fourth section) and radio controls (fifth section). The RS-2U weighed 184 pounds (83.5 kg), had a speed of 1,025 mph (1,650 kmh) and the warhead was equipped with a proximity fuse.

The AA-1 Alkali was equipped with a simple semi-active radar guidance system that homed on the reflected radar energy from the beam generated by the carrier aircraft. If the RS-2U did not hit the target after twenty-three seconds of flight, it would self-destruct. The rocket motor had a burn time of 5.5 seconds. When the proximity fuse detonated the warhead close to the target, the explosion produced some 830 fragments, enough to shred most targets.

Since the AA-1 Alkali was a beam rider, the MiG-19PM pilot had to illuminate the target until missile impact. Any evasive maneuvers would break the lock-on and the missile would go ballistic. Multiple missiles could be launched using the same illumination beam. Test

A MiG-19PM Farmer E, Blue 05, of a PVO air defense unit, climbs out on another interception sortie. The aircraft carries four APU-4 missile rails for RS-2U (AA-1 Alkali) air-to-air beam rider guided missiles as well as two 200 gallon (760 liter) underwing tanks. (A. A. Zirnov)

A late Soviet MiG-19PM of a PVO air defense regiment. The aircraft is equipped with a Syrena 2 tail warning radar received above the position light on the fin tip. The Syrena 2 system was introduced on late production batches of the Farmer E and was only used on Soviet aircraft. The aircraft is armed with four RS-2U (NATO reporting name AA-1 Alkali) beam riding air-to-air missiles on the APU-4 missile rails. The AA-1 had a speed of 1,025 mph and was equipped with a proximity fuse warhead. (A.A. Zirnov)

Weapons System Development

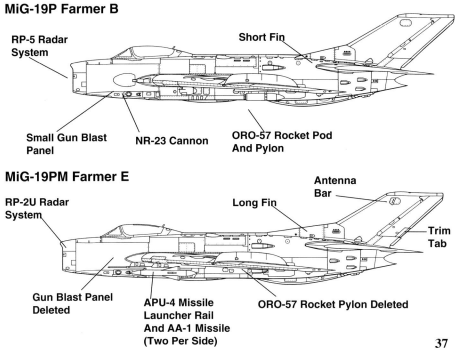

A late production MiG-19PM Farmer E with a Syrena 2 tail warning radar receiver antenna on the fin tip parked in front of a hardened aircraft shelter on a Soviet air base. The national insignia was also applied on the wing uppersurface and the aircraft's tactical number, Blue 30, was repeated on the 200 gallon (760 liter) underwing fuel tanks. (A.A. Zirnov)

(Below) An East German MiG-19PM, Red 512, (Serial Number 650930) is refueled prior to another mission over the German Democratic Republic during 1962. The aircraft later cashed on 20 October 1962 during a night interception mission. At the time of the crash, the aircraft was being flown by LT Roland Rössner who brought the aircraft down near Meissen on the Elbe river. (Hans-Georg Volprich)

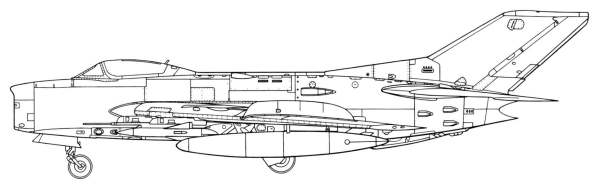

Specification

MiG-19PM Farmer E

Wingspan	30 feet 2 inches (9.1 m)
Length	48 feet 4 inches (14.63 m)
Height	12 feet 0 inches (2.97 m)
Empty Weight	11,464 pounds (5,200 kg)
Maximum Weight	20,062 pounds (9,160 kg)
Power plant	Two 7,165 lbst RD-9B afterburning turbojet engines
Armament	Four AA-1 Alkali missiles
Speed	898 mph (1,445 kph)
Service Ceiling	53,899 feet (16,800 m)
Range	1,187 miles (1,910 km)
Crew	One

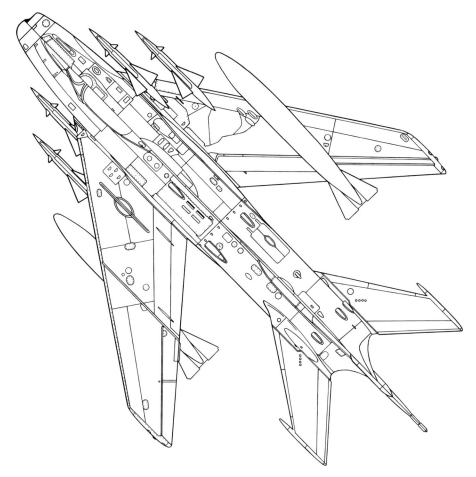

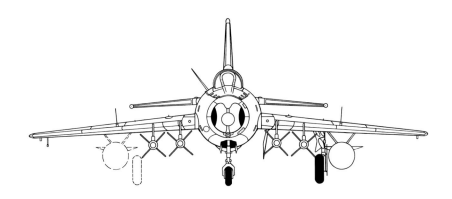

A line-up of MiG-19PM Farmer Es and MiG-19S Farmer Cs of *Jagdfliegergeschwader 3* at Preschen in the German Democratic Republic. The Farmer Es were assigned to the 2nd Squadron, while the MiG-19S Farmer Cs were assigned to the 1st Squadron. The MiG-19PM in the foreground, Red 391, now serves as a gate guard at Preschen AFB. (Hans-Georg Volprich)

A Polish MiG-19PM, Red 917, being readied for a mission from Slupsk-Redzikowo near the Baltic coast. All Polish MiG-19PMs carried three digit Red unoutlined tactical numbers. During the training missions, the APU-4 missile rails were carried, although the AA-1 Alkali missiles were not carried as a safety precaution. (Zolnierz Polski via Andrzej Morgala)

revealed that the AA-1 Alkali could be used with some success against large, cumbersome aircraft, such as four engine bombers, but the chances to score a kill against a fast, maneuvering fighter type target were very low.

There were a number of differences between the MiG-19P and MiG-91PM. While the MiG-19P was equipped with the RP-5 radar system, which was optimized for gun armament, the MiG-19PM used the RP-2U system intended for missile illumination.

The RP-2U radar system was quite similar to the RP-5 Scan Odd except that it had an increased scan range (2,000 meter for the RP-5 and 3,500 meter for the RP-2U). A Green light was installed in the cockpit that flashed when the target was between 3,500 and 1,500 meters. A Red lamp flashed when the target was within 2,000 meters, which was too close for a successful missile firing. Both, the RP-2U and the RP-5 radar system had serious opera-

This jacked up East German Air Force MiG-19PM, Red 391, is having its radar systems checked by electronics technicians. A workstand with test equipment has been set up next to the nose. While the radar is being tested, other maintenance personnel are working on systems within the fuselage. (Hans-Georg Volprich)

(Right) This was a stage event designed to confuse NATO intelligence during 1965 at the Sea Days Celebrations at Gdynia. A number of 28th Fighter Regiment MiG-19PMs were sent to that base and were photographed being worked on by Naval personnel in order to make NATO observers believe that Polish Navy Regiments were equipped with Farmer Es. (Wojciech Luczak)

A Polish Air Force MiG-19PM Farmer E, Red 905, on the ramp of the home base of the 28th Fighter Regiment. Some of the differences between the MiG-19P and the MiG-19PM were the long fin extension, the antenna bar on top of the vertical fin and the trim tab fitted to the rudder. (Andrzei Morgala)

The MiG-19PM cockpit had a SS-45-1-100-OS gun sight camera mounted on the upper canopy framing. Below it was the ASP-5-NV-V reflector gun sight, to the right of the gun sight was the AR-18-4 radar scope for the RP-2U radar system. The radar screen was equipped with a hood for use in daylight. (Andrzej Morgala)

A MiG-19PM Farmer E is towed along the ramp at Slupsk-Redzikowo air base by a Polish-built STAR truck. All Polish Air Force Farmers carried the national insignia on th fuselage side, fin and wing undersurfaces. Polish aircraft did not carry the national insignia on the wing uppersurfaces. (Andrzej Morgala)

An overall Natural Metal MiG-19PM Farmer E of the *28. Pulk Lotnictwa Mysliwskiego* (28th Fighter Regiment) on its hardstand at Slupsk-Redzikowo on a rainy day. The Farmer Es in the background are all fitted with Red air intake covers. (Andrzej Morgala)

tional shortcomings and a large number of MiG-19P and MiG-19PMs were grounded for a long periods, because of defective radar systems. These systems were also difficult to maintain at squadron levels. The two NR-23 cannon and their blast panels were deleted and two underwing pylons with BD-3-56 universal bomb racks were installed on each wing. These pylons were fitted with APU-4 launch rails for the AA-1 Alkali air-to-air missiles, giving the MiG-19PM a total missile load of four weapons. The pylons were also fitted with the OS-4 wiring system which insured the proper connection of electrical power and heating for the vital component of the missile.

The MiG-19PM could carry, in place of the AA-1s, four unguided ARS-160 or ARS-212M rockets. These two types of rockets were intended for use against surface targets, and were rarely carried on the MiG-19PM. While the MiG-19S and MiG-19P could carry an ORO-57K pod on a pylon mounted behind the main wheel bay, this provision was deleted on the MiG-19PM.

A number of modifications were also introduced in the tail section. While all MiG-19Ps had the short fin extension, a carry over from the early MiG-19S Farmer C, all MiG-19PMs had the long fin extension found on the late production MiG-19S. An antenna bar was added on both sides of the upper fin and a rudder trim tab was added. Originally, the MiG-19P was not equipped with a trim tab, but some Farmer Bs were retrofitted with the trim tab as a field modification.

All MiG-19Ps and the main production batches of the MiG-19PM were not equipped with a Syrena 2 tail warning system; however, some late production batches were equipped with the Syrena 2 system which was mounted above the position light on the fin tip. The antenna fitted to the MiG-19PM was much more conical in shape than the antenna carried on the earlier MiG-19S. The Syrena 2 was only used on Soviet MiG-19PMs, those aircraft exported had the system removed before export. There were about 250 MiG-19PMs built at GAZ 21 before production was phased out in late 1957 in favor of the more advanced MiG-21F-13 Fishbed.

MiG-19PMs were exported to all Warsaw Pact countries; however, only a few of these were new production aircraft. The majority of the MiG-19PMs were ex-Soviet Air Force aircraft.

The first MiG-19PM were delivered to Warsaw Pact satellites from 1959 onward. Czechoslovakia received thirty-three MiG-19PM between 1959 to 1960. These aircraft came from Soviet Air Force stocks and were given the designation S-106. In September of 1958, even before the first MiG-19PM arrived, a delegation departed for the Soviet Union to discuss the establishment of a MiG-19PM production line in Czechoslovakia. It was planned to produce some 430 aircraft at the Aero Company, however the plan was dropped during the Summer of 1959 and no MiG-19PMs were in fact produced in Czechoslovakia.

On 5 September 1958, the German Democratic Republic (East Germany) signed a contract for twelve MiG-l9PMs for the contract price of 17.25 Million Marks. Pilots and ground crew received their conversion training at Savaslaika in the Soviet Union. At Krasnovodsk on the Caspian Sea, the crews received life fire missile training against drones released by Tu-4 Bull (B-29 Superfortress copies). On 20 October 1959 the MiG-19PMs were turned over to the *1. Staffel* (1st Squadron) of the *Jagdfliegergesobwader 3* (3rd Fighter Regiment). In early 1961 the unit reported that it was operationally ready. By this time, the MiG-19PM had earned a very bad reputation within the 3rd Fighter Regiment and many aircraft were grounded because of defective RP-2U radar systems and other mechanical and technical failures. During a very short time, four MiG-19PM were lost, some under very mysterious conditions and the type soon earned the reputation as a "Widow Maker" in East Germany. On 16 December 1961 the first East German Farmer, flown by 1st LT Lauterbach was lost. This was a MiG-19PM (Serial 650928) Red 754. Another MiG-19PM was lost on 28 July 1962 and still another was lost on 28 June 1964. In May of 1969, all remaining MiG-19PMs were retired from East

A MiG-19PM Farmer E, Red 37, of the *31. Honi Vadaszrepülö Ezred* (31st Home Defense Interceptor Regiment), Hungarian Air Force. There were a total of twelve Farmer Es supplied to the Hungarian Air Force during 1959. (George Punka)

German service.

After the Hungarian revolution of October 1956 the *Magyar Legierö* (Hungarian Air Force) was disbanded and the Soviets confiscated all aircraft. In June of 1959 President Khrushchev visited the Hungarian Metropole Budapest and found that the Kadar regime was strong and reliable. For this reason he authorized the establishment of a new Hungarian Air Force was permitted. Part of the aircraft transferred to the new air arm were twelve MiG-19PM Farmer Es. In July of 1959 training for twelve Hungarian pilots was started in the Soviet Union, initially on the MiG-19P, but later on the MiG-19PM. Hungarian pilots also performed live missile training over the Kara-Kum desert in the Soviet Union. Flying targets were released by Tu-4 Bull bombers and the Hungarian pilots had to intercept and destroy them with the AA-1 Alkali missiles. The first six MiG-19PMs were delivered to Taszar in March of 1960 and a further six followed in April of that same year. These aircraft were all allocated to the 3rd

This Hungarian Air Force MiG-19PM, Red 35, was the first aircraft of this type to be lost in Hungary. It crashed on 24 October 1964 near Mesztegnyö, killing the pilot, MAJ Bela Bognar. All Hungarian MiG-19PMs were overall Natural Metal with Red tactical numbers with thin White outlines. (George Punka)

The bar-antenna on the tail-fin and the trim tab clearly identify this as a MiG-19PM Farmer E. The Farmer E differed from the Farmer C in that it had three staggered cooling air inlets on the rear fuselage while the MiG-19S had three air inlets in a vertical line. (Andrzej Morgala)

This badly damaged MiG-19PM (Serial Number 1136.) once served as Red 36 in the Hungarian Air Force. The White outlined tactical number, Red 1978, denotes the year the aircraft became a display subject. The Farmer E now rests at Veces storage depot, awaiting restoration. (Johann Sauberzweig)

Pilot and ground crew men scramble to a MiG-19PM Farmer E, Red 37, (Serial Number 6510371) of the Hungarian Air Force during an exercise at Taszar Air Force Base. The Farmer E is equipped with an RS-2U (AA-1 Alkali) missile on the outboard missile pylon. (Hadtorteneti Museum via Attila Bonhardt)

Squadron of the *31. Honi Vadaszrepülö Ezred* (31st Home Defense Interceptor Regiment) based at Taszar. Two digit, White outlined tactical numbers, Red 27 to Red 38 were issued to these aircraft. The tactical numbers were the last two digits of the serial number (651027 to 651038). On 4 April 1961 the MiG-19PM was introduced to the public, when a formation of three Farmer Es, Red 32, Red 31 and Red 38 took part in a fly over during a military parade. The night interception tactics learned by the Hungarian Farmer pilots were based on experience gained by this country during the Second World War with the Messerschmitt Bf 110 night-fighter. Hungarian tactics were all based on German Luftwaffe tactics rather than Soviet tactics. Three aircraft crashed during operational service; the first loss occurred on 24 October 1964 when a MiG-19PM, Red 35, crashed near Mesztegnyo killing the pilot MAJ Bela Bognar. MAJ Zsigmond Vass was killed flying a MiG-19PM, Red 29, on 19 February 1968 when the aircraft crashed near a farmhouse at Agusztin-Tanya. On 16 September 1970, a MiG-19PM, Red 38, crashed on the final approach at Taszar, although the pilot, CAPT Istvan Bako survived the incident. In 1974 the surviving MiG-19PMs were retired from active service.

In 1959, the first MiG-19PMs were delivered to a single *Eskadra* (Squadron) the 28th Fighter Regiment at Slupsk-Redzikowo where they served together with the MiG-19P. Only one other Polish unit was equipped with the type, the 39th Fighter Regiment at Mierzecice. A Poles operated a total of twenty-five MiG-19P and MiG-19PM. Ten were assigned to each squadron, while five were held as an operational reserve. During 1966 and 1967 the 39th Fighter Regiment was re-equipped with the MiG-21PF and all remaining MiG-19Ps and MiG-19PMs were either exported to Bulgaria or transferred to the 28th Regiment. All Polish MiG-19P and MiG-19PM were withdrawn from service in 1976.

In 1959 a total of forty-five MiG-19PM were delivered to *Divizia 66 Aviatie Vinatoare* (66th Fighter Regiment) of the Romanian Air Force. Initially these Farmers were all based at Deveselul Air Force Base, but later the unit moved to Boreca Air Force Base. In 1960 some of these were used to bolster the air defense squadron based at Timisoara Air Force Base in Transylvania. Initially the MiG-19PMs received tactical numbers ranging from Red 016 to Red 060. In 1965, the first digit of the tactical number was changed to 7 and shortly before they were retired, the aircraft had the tactical number change again with the first digit becoming 8. When the MiG-21F-13 became available in Rumania, the Farmers were withdrawn from front-line service. The last MiG-19PMs were withdrawn during mid-1970.

In October of 1959 a dozen MiG-19PMs were supplied to the *Forcat Ushtarake Ajore Shgipetare* (Albanian Air Force) to equip Regiment 7594 based at Rinas Air Force Base, northwest of the capital Tirana. In 1965, these aircraft were sent to China in exchange for a like number of Shenyang F-6 day fighters.

The last Warsaw Pact country to receive the MiG-19PM was Bulgaria, which received twelve ex-Polish Air Force MiG-19PMs during 1967. These saw service with a single squadron the 19th Fighter Regiment at Graf Ignatievo. These aircraft were all withdrawn from service in 1975.

This MiG-19PM Farmer E, Red 020, was one of forty-five Farmer Es assigned to the 66th Fighter Division based at Boreca Air Force Base, Rumania. A distinctive feature of all Romanian Farmers was the painting of the wing root in Black. (Dan Antoniu)

Shenyang J-6/F-6

Shenyang J-6 Farmer C

In May of 1953, an agreement between the Soviet Union and China set the stage for the production of Soviet aircraft in China. The agreement called for the Soviets to provide technical assistance to the Chinese Aviation Industry. Several Soviet aircraft were selected for license production in the People's Republic of China. This was the first step toward forming an indigenous aviation industry in China.

When the production line for the MiG-19 was closed in the Soviet Union during late 1957, the Soviets granted a license to manufacture the type in China and in January of 1958 the first drawings and technical information were supplied to the Shenyang National Aircraft Factory. Shenyang was already engaged in license production of the J-5 (MiG-17F Fresco C).

In contrast to the J-5 program, where the Soviets supplied massive technical support, the Soviets supplied only engineering drawings and technical documentation. No jigs or other tooling machines were supplied. The only hardware received was five MiG-19PMs, which arrived in a knocked-down condition.

The first MiG-19 variant to be produced was the MiG-19P Farmer B and the first Chinese assembled example took off for its maiden flight on 17 December 1958 with test pilot Wang Youhuai at the control. The type was certified for mass production by the State Certification Committee in April of 1959 under the designation J-6 (J for Jianjiji or Fighter).

The Soviet RD-9B power plant was built under license with the designation WP-6 at the Shenyang Aeroengine Factory and the Chengdu Aeroengine Factory. The first documents for these engines arrived from the Soviet Union during early 1958. Initially the Chinese could not produce these engines due to their sophisticated design. When compared to the earlier the WP-5 (Soviet Klimov VK-1F) power plant, the RD-9B was much more complex. It consisted of 2,521 parts, some forty-six percent more than the WP-5. An axial-flow engine with magnesium parts and precision castings were well beyond Chinese aero-engine manufacturing standards at this time. By end of 1960, no WP-6 engines had been accepted for service by the People's Liberation Army due to their poor manufacturing quality.

This Chinese J-6, Red 51887, has been fitted with an unidentified container on the fuselage centerline in front of the ventral fin. The curved pilot boarding ladder is a locally designed item. (Josef Simon)

This Chinese-built J-6 (MiG-19S), Red 50594, has a Red-Orange fin tip. The aircraft is assigned to the 38th Air Division which has the task of air defense for the Chinese capital of Beijing. (Josef Simon)

In January of 1959, President Khrushchev and Foreign Minister Gromyko visited China. Shortly after this visit, Sino-Soviet relations began to deteriorate and in July of 1960, all economic and technical aid was halted. As a result, all 1,390 Soviet experts and advisors were recalled. Since the western nations continued to enforce trade embargoes against China and the Soviets had withdrawn their support, all technological advancements for the Chinese aviation industry came to a complete standstill.

For the young Chinese aviation industry this immense blow was compounded by the unhealthy influence of the "Great Leap Forward" which started in May of 1958. Under this program the Chinese leadership demanded that as civil and military goods should be produced in quaintly, as regardless of their quality.

As a result of the inferior quality of the J-6 Farmer B built at the Shenyang factory the Air Force refused to accept these aircraft and production came to a halt. Finally, the necessary measures were taken in to improve the manufacturing quality of the J-6. As part of this, a decision was made to cancel production of the MiG-19P in favor of the MiG-19S. Technical documentation for the Farmer C had been received shortly before the cooperation program with the Soviet Union had ended.

Prototype production of the MiG-19S under the designation J-6 began during 1961 after the production and master tooling had been rebuilt and improved. In December of 1963 the J-6 was certified for mass production by the State Certification Committee and the first production examples were allocated to the 38th Air Division which was responsible for defending

This Chinese-built F-6, Black 1817, was assigned to No. 15 Squadron, Cobras, at Peshawar Air Base, Pakistan. The F-6 is now being withdrawn from front-line service, although a few F-6s are allocated for airfield defense at every Pakistani Air Force Base because of their high rate of climb. (Peter Steinemann)

Fuselage Development

MiG-19S Farmer C

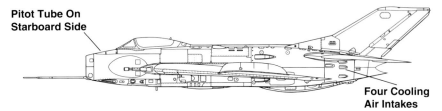

Shenyang J-6

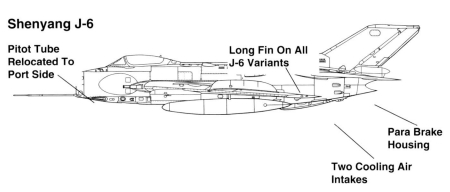

Beijing.

Based on the fact that the initial production of the J-6 was based on the MiG-19P, this had also some influence on MiG-19S production. The only external difference between a Soviet and a Chinese manufactured MiG-19S were the number and position of the cooling air inlets on the rear fuselage and the position of the pitot tube. The MiG-19S had four cooling inlets three of them arranged vertically in line, while the J-6 had two intakes which were slightly staggered. Most J-6s had the pitot tube on the port side in front of the canopy, while all Soviet-built Farmer Cs had the pitot tube on the starboard side. A Farmer C can be assumed to be Chinese-built if the pitot tube is on the port side.

The Shenyang Aircraft Factory also improved production techniques and made some improvements to the Farmer itself. Most J-6s were equipped with a weapons pylon mounted on the wing forward edge, similar to the pylon carried on East German Farmer Cs. This pylon was used primarily for rocket pods, but it could also carry small bombs.

Late production batches featured a unique modification, found only on Chinese built J-6s. The braking parachute container was relocated from the port side rear fuselage to bullet shaped container at the base of the fin and rudder. This modification was undertaken during regular overhauls and proved to be very practical. Later, the MiG Design Bureau used this system when it developed the MiG-21PFM, mounted the braking parachute in a similar container at the base of the rudder.

A total of some 4,500 J-6s were built at the Shenyang factory, more than had been produced in the Soviet Union. Even in the early 1990s there were still some 800 J-6s allocated to Air Defense Regiments and another 1,200 assigned to strike units of Chung-Kuo Shan Min Taie Fang Tsun Pu-Tai (Air Force of the People's Liberation Army), plus another 300 Farmer Cs serving with the Chinese Navy.

The J-6 was still under production in 1986, some 25 years after production of the Farmer C was first launched at Shenyang. One of the main reasons for this long production duration was that with the loss of Soviet assistance and the Western technology embargo, China lagged years behind in scientific research and this slowed development and mass production of a new generation aircraft, such as the J-7 (MiG-21 Fishbed copy). Until the mid-1970s, the J-6 was the only interceptor which could be produced in numbers by the People's Republic of China.

This overall White Pakistani F-6 of No 19 Squadron carries a locally designed belly tank under the fuselage. Although of Pakistani design it was also adopted by the Chinese Air Force. The small aerial on the upper nose is another Pakistani modification. Additionally, the wing root cannons do not have gun gas defectors on the gun muzzle. (Peter Steinemann)

Three overall Natural Metal Pakistani F-6s of No 15 Squadron, Cobras in 'V' formation near the famous Khyber pass. Only the aircraft in the foreground has the bullet shaped braking parachute container at the base of the rudder, the other two F-6s, Black 3311 and Black 1817, are early production aircraft and have yet to be retrofitted with the container. All three have been fitted with an additional wing pylon to accommodate an American AIM-9 Sidewinder missile outboard of the 200 gallon underwing fuel tanks. The Pakistani F-6s are the only F-6s to feature this modification. The pylons are installed in Pakistani during regular overhaul. All aircraft carry Red turbine warning stripes on the rear fuselage, ejection seat warning triangles under the cockpit and have the tactical number repeated on the nose and rear fuselage in Black. (Peter Steinemann)

Pakistani Farmer Modifications

Shenyang J-6

Shenyang F-6 (Pakistani Modifications)

The People's Republic of China is divided into eight Military Air Regions. The command structure is organized on a regional basis, rather than by functional commands. Each Air Division has up to 120 fighter aircraft, assigned to three Regiments, each with three Brigades of 15 aircraft each. The structure of a Chinese Air Division was taken from the Soviet Air Force and at its peak more than 40 Regiments were equipped with the J-6.

In the 1960s and early 1970s the J-6 was the backbone of Chinese air defense units. In 1964 and 1965 two RF-101 Voodoos were shot down by Chinese J-6s and in 1965 an F-104 Starfighter became a victim of a Navy J-6. In 1967, two U.S. Navy A-6 Intruders were shot down by two Air Force Farmer C when they strayed over Hinan Island in the Gulf of Tonkin. According Chinese reports, a total of fourteen foreign aircraft were shot down while attempting to violate Chinese airspace.

Chinese J-6s were also deployed to the Sino-Soviet border after the clashes between Soviet and Chinese border troops on Damansky Island during 1969. A few J-6s took also part on the ill fated Chinese invasion of Vietnam in February of 1979.

Five J-6 pilots of the People's Liberation Army have successfully defected to Taiwan or South Korea between July 1977 and November of 1987. These defections took place, regardless of the fact that, the SAM-batteries of the People's Liberation Army placed along the Chinese coast were not only intended to shot down "imperialist" intruders, but also friendly aircraft with "freedom seekers" on board. On 7 July 1977 Squadron Leader Fan Yuanyen touched down his J-6, Red 3171 at Tainan AFB on Formosa and became the first Chinese

A two tone Gray camouflaged F-6 of No 19 Squadron, Pakistani Air Force. The aircraft is a late production F-6 with Pakistani modifications including the deletion of the antenna mast under the cockpit and the addition of AIM-9 Sidewinder rails on the outboard wing panels. The under fuselage speed brake is in the deployed position. (Peter Steinemann)

This F-6 of No 15 Squadron, Cobras, was based at Peshawar Air Base. Peshawar was the base from which Gary Powers launched his ill-fated U-2 mission over the Soviet Union. The checker board design on the nose, air data boom and rudder are Black and White., while the tips of the 200 gallon underwing tanks and Sidewinder missile rails are in Red. (Peter Steinemann)

A pair of F-6s of the Combat Commanders School fly over the Swat hills near Sargodha, Pakistan. Both of these aircraft are armed with AIM-9P Sidewinder infrared homing air-to-air missiles on the outboard wing pylons. (Peter Steinemann)

Farmer pilot to successfully defect to the West. He was followed by Wu Jung-ken, flying Red 3220, who defected to the South Korean airstrip of K-16 near Seoul on 16 October 1982. On 21 February 1986, a 26 year old F-6 pilot, Chen Pao-chung left a formation of J-6s during a combat training mission and headed for Suwon Air Force Base in South Korea. While his J-6, Red 3280, remained in Korea, the pilot was transferred to Taiwan. On 24 October 1986 ,Squadron Leader Jeng Tsai-tien of the 15th Naval Air Regiment defected to Ching-Jon aerodrome in South Korea and on 19 November 1987, Liu Chih-yuan of the 145th Aviation Regiment left a formation of four J-6s and landed at Ching Chuan Kang Air Base in Nationalist China.

Shenyang JZ-6 Reconnaissance Variant

During 1966 the Shenyang Aircraft factory began to modify the J-6 to fill the tactical reconnaissance role by installing optical cameras for day and an infrared scanning camera for night missions. Small scale production was started in 1967 with the designation JZ-6.

The type was continuously developed and in 1971 a version of the JZ-6 for high altitude missions was developed. In 1975, another variant was developed to perform both high and low altitude missions.

Shenyang J-6A

The Nanchang Aircraft Factory was assigned the task of license production of the MiG-19P Farmer B and MiG-19PM Farmer D. The first prototype assembled at Nanchang made its first flight on 28 September 1959, with Wang Youhuai at the controls. There were only seven aircraft produced before production was closed because of quality shortcomings. The WP-6 power plant for the radar equipped version of the J-6 had been built at the Zhuzhou Aero Engine Factory.

In March of 1959 production of the MiG-19PM was started. Earlier, the Soviet Union had

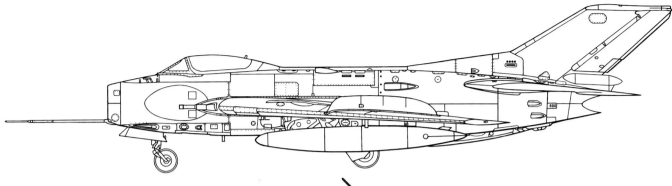

Specification

Shenyang F-6 Farmer C

Wingspan	30 feet 2 inches (9.1 m)
Length	46 feet 11 inches (14.32 m)
Height	12 feet (2.97 m)
Empty Weight	12,699 pounds (5,760 kg)
Maximum Weight	22,046 pounds (10,000 kg)
Power plant	Two 7,165 lbst Wopen 6 afterburning turbojet engines
Armament	Three NR-30 30mm cannons.
Speed	903 mph (1,453 kph)
Service Ceiling	58,725 feet (17,900 m)
Range	1,243 miles (2,000 km)
Crew	One

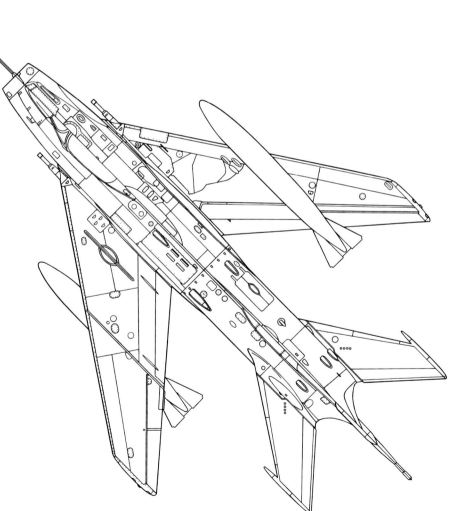

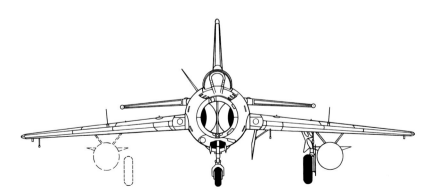

A line-up of ex-Pakistani F-6s of No 25 Squadron, Bangladeshi Air Force on the ramp at Chittagong-Patenga Air Base. The aircraft in the foreground, Black 901, has early style N-30 cannons with gun gas defectors on the muzzle and retains the antenna mast under the cockpit. (Peter Steinemann)

Black 901 on the ramp at Chittagong-Patenga Air Base, Bangladesh. The F-6s operated by Bangladesh are all rebuilt ex-Pakistani Air Force aircraft. Before they were delivered to Bangladesh the aircraft were refurbished, and the outboard AIM-9 Sidewinder missile pylon and its wiring was deleted. This aircraft is armed with two seven shot 55MM rocket pods on the underwing weapons pylon. The tactical number on the nose consists of the last three numbers of the aircraft's serial which is carried on the rear fuselage in Black. (Peter Steinemann)

This Bangladeshi F-6, Black 7104, is armed with seven shot rocket pods and carries two 200 gallon (760 liter) underwing fuel tanks. It is a late production F-6 with the bullet shaped braking parachute container at the base of the rudder and N-30 cannons without gun gas defectors on the muzzles. (Peter Steinemann)

supplied five MiG-19PM as knocked down kits plus all drawings and technical documentation needed for production. Another nineteen examples were manufactured at Nanchang Aircraft Factory.

The AA-1 Alkali missile armament for the MiG-19PM was produced under the designation PL-1 at the Zhuzhou Aeroengine Factory and the first factory trials were started in the second half of 1958. After a number of setbacks and efforts at improving the manufacturing quality, the PL-1 was cleared for mass production in April of 1964.

Small scale production of the J-6A all-weather fighter with its armament of four AA-1 missiles begun during 1977.

Export Shenyang F-6

The J-5 had been exported to a number of foreign countries under the designation F-5 (F for Fighter). There is a sharp contrast between inflexible Soviet export policies and the way the Chinese export military equipment. In the Soviet Union the export of state of art aircraft is only allowed with downgraded avionics or other equipment. No individual customer requirements regarding equipment and avionics are generally accepted. The Chinese export industry cares for the needs of the customer and, as a result, Western equipment or non-standard Chinese items can be built into the aircraft on the production line in China or modified after delivery according the customer's requirements.

One of the first foreign customer of the F-6 was Pakistan. With the beginning of a twenty-two days long Indian-Pakistani war in September of 1965, the U.S. government suspended all military aid and sales to both India and Pakistan. The embargo hardly affected India, whose defense infrastructure had since long been adapted to Soviet technology and production tech-

A early production F-6 Farmer C of Regiment 1875, Albanian Air Force on the ramp at Berat-Kucove Air Base during the early 1990s. The aircraft's tactical number, Red 4-03, is repeated on the underwing tanks and the unguided rocket on the inboard pylon. (Achille Vigna)

This Albanian F-6, Red 8-23, of Regiment 5646 based at Lezha-Zadrima Air Base. The first digit of the tactical number identifies the aircraft's unit assignment, in this case the 8 stands for Regiment 5646. Reportedly Albania is changing its national markings from the star in circle to a Red rectangle with a Black double headed eagle superimposed over the rectangle. (Achille Vigna)

A late production F-6 of the Egyptian Air Force on the ramp at Cairo West Air Base during exercise *Bright Star '83*. There were two units equipped with the F-6, No. 242 Brigade at Beni Suef and No 241 Brigade at Bielbeis East. Some forty F-6s were shipped through Egypt to Iraq during the Iran/Iraq war, along with a number of F-7s (Chinese MiG-21s). The aircraft in the background are USAF C-130s. (Dick Cole)

niques, but it had a devastating effect on the Pakistan Air Force, which had previously acquired all its front-line aircraft, such as the F-86 and the F-104 from the United States.

Negotiations with the People's Republic of China started in October of 1965. Pakistani pilots were sent to China in order to perform minimal flight conversion and technical courses. All the operational manuals had to be painstakingly translated word for word from the Chinese lettering into the English language.

The first sixty F-6 were donated to Pakistan by the People's Republic of China and the first examples were ferried from Hotan in China by Pakistani pilots in late December of 1965. These fighters were used to equip No 25 Eagles Squadron at Sargodha and the aircraft were introduced to the public during the Republic Day Parade in March of 1966. All the aircraft of the first batch delivered to Pakistan lacked the braking parachute housing at the base of the rudder and all had the Soviet type gun deflector ring fitted on the NR-30 cannon. They were all delivered in an overall Natural Metal finish. The donation of sixty F-6s shortly after the Indian-Pakistani war 1965 was prompted by the fact that China was also having border problems with India and assisting Pakistan took some of the pressure off the border area.

The F-6 also played an important role in both the air defense and ground support roles during the Indian-Pakistani conflict of 1971. On the morning of 4 December the Indian Air Force launched a large scale strike against Pakistani airfields with some seventy Hunters and Su-7s. The F-6s proved to be highly successful and two Pakistani pilots. FLT LT K. Latif managed to shoot down a Su-7 Fitter A, while another pilot, FLT LT Sarfraz damaged a Su-7. That same day, FLT LT J. Qazi clobbered a Hunter over Mianwali — the first kills for Pakistani F-6s. The devastating punch of the three 30MM cannons of the F-6s was evident during close support missions on 4 December in the Chamb-Jaurian sector where eighteen medium guns and an ammunition dump were destroyed. Close support missions by F-6s continued to be flown throughout the entire conflict.

On 7 December 1971, FLT LTs Atig and Mushaf met four Indian Su-7s and downed two of them. But the war was not one sided and on 7 December an F-6 flown by FLT LT Wajid Ali

Egyptian Air Force F-6s carried an unusual air superiority camouflage consisting of a two tone Gray uppersurface pattern over Light Gray undersides. The tactical number was carried on the nose in Black Arabic numbers. (Dick Cole)

was hit by flak and the pilot became a POW. On 11 December LT Shahid Raza's F-6 also became a victim of enemy anti-aircraft fire.

In early 1972, a rebuild factory for the F-6s was donated by the Chinese and erected at the Pakistan Aeronautical Complex at Kamra. Before the establishment of this facility the F-6s had to be shipped to China for airframe overhaul, which usually took between twenty months

This Khmer Rouge Air Force (Kampuchea/Cambodia) F-6, Red 30-950, is being towed across the ramp by a Vietnamese Army truck shortly after the Vietnamese invaded Kampuchea during the Spring of 1979. This particular aircraft is now in storage at the Army Museum at Phnom Phen, Cambodia. (A.J. Walg Collection)

North Korean pilots discuss combat tactics in the grass next to the ramp at a North Korean Base. The aircraft in the background is a late production F-6. NKAF F-6s were overall Natural Metal with the national insignia carried in six positions and Red tactical numbers on the nose. (Wojciech Luezak).

and two years. Formal commissioning of the factory took place on 8 November 1980. Kamra also developed a 301 gallon (1,140 liter) belly tank for the F-6. This drop tank was intended to replace the two underwing tanks normally carried, freeing up these stations for other ordnance. The tank was so successful that it was adopted by the Chinese Air Force. Spare parts were manufactured as well as forgings and castings for the F-6. Only forty percent of the needed spare parts are imported from China, while the rest are manufactured locally.

Another 125 F-6s have been supplied to Pakistan at very favorable prices. Deliveries of these aircraft began during 1978 and, in contrast with the initial batch, these aircraft were fit-

Black 460, a late production F-6 of the *Dayuuradaha Xoogga Dalka Somaliyeed* (Somali Aeronautical Corps), lies abandoned on the aircraft dump at Modadishu Airport. The aircraft had been stripped of all useful items by the gangs that roamed Somali after the civil war ended. At one time the SAC had operated some twenty-four F-6 and TF-6 Farmers. (Paul Jackson)

ted with the drag chute container at the base of the rudder.

Pakistani F-6s served with Nos 15, 17, 23 and 25 Squadrons. Pakistani Air Force F-6s had a number of differences between them and the original J-6. The ejection seat was replaced by a British Martin-Baker Mk PKD 10 seat. The starboard antenna mast below the cockpit was deleted and replaced by an aerial mounted on the starboard side of the nose. Pakistani F-6s are also equipped with an additional wing pylon to accommodate the American AIM-9 Sidewinder air-to-air missile. This feature is unique to Pakistani F-6s and was introduced at the overhaul facility at Kamra.

The F-6s are being slowly withdrawn from front-line service and are being replaced by F-16s and the F-7P Skybolt. But due to its high rate of climb, a number of F-6s have been retained and assigned for air base protection at every major Pakistani air base.

North Vietnam received a number of F-6s during the Vietnam war. During late 1965 a number of Vietnamese instructors and pilots were sent to China for training and the first F-6s were delivered to North Vietnam during 1966. Additional examples were delivered after the 1968 bombing halt. The number of North Vietnamese Farmer Cs was always low and never exceeded forty aircraft. Most of the F-6 were allocated to the 3rd Company of the North Vietnamese Air Force

The first clashes between USAF aircraft and F-6s North Vietnam begun when the air war over North Vietnam was resumed in May of 1972, under the code name Linebacker I.

The first F-6 fell to USAF pilots on 8 May 1972; when MAJ Barton P. Crews and his backseater CAPT Keith W. Jones Jr., of the 13th TFS launched a Sparrow against a Farmer C northwest of Hanoi.

But USAF pilots over southeast Asia quickly learned that the F-6 was far from a "sitting duck" in combat. Due to its high rate of climb and good acceleration, added to the hitting power of three 30MM cannon, the aircraft was ideally suited for the "hit and run" tactics used by the North Vietnamese Air Force.

The leading USAF MiG killer team over Vietnam was lost to the Farmer. On 10 May 1972 during a weather reconnaissance mission for the Paul Doumer Bridge attack force MAJ Bob Lodge and CAPT Roger Locher of the 432nd TRW were hit by cannon fire from two North Vietnamese F-6. The Phantom was badly hit and MAJ Lodge was killed but CAPT Locher ejected and was rescued after evading capture for some twenty-three days. That same day, another F-4E of the 432nd was shot down by F-6 cannon fire. The crew, CAPT J. Harris and CAPT D. Wikinson were killed. Two North Vietnamese aces, Le Thanh Dao and Ngyuyen Doc Soat claimed some, if not all of their kills during the Linebacker I campaign while flying F-6s. The North Vietnamese pilots usually endeavored to fight on their own terms, engaging in snap attacks and braking off the engagement when the element of surprise was lost.

The Peoples Republic of Bangladesh received its first of twenty-four F-6s during 1978. These aircraft were delivered from Pakistani stocks. They were assigned to No 8 Squadron and to No 25 Squadron both based at Chittagong-Patenga Air Base. This batch was followed by a second batch of sixteen F-6s. A substantial number of aircraft at this base were destroyed during a 140 mph cyclone which hit Bangladesh on 30 April 1991. The Bangladeshi Air Force F-6s carry the same two tone Gray camouflage as Pakistani Farmer Cs with the Black tactical numbers applied on the nose and on the fin.

Another Asian user of the F-6 was Cambodia (also known as Kampuchea). In 1964 Prince Norodom Sihanouk visited China and as a result of this trip, the Khmer Air Force took delivery of a number of F-5 Fresco Cs. The victory of the Communists in Vietnam during early 1975 and the subsequent border clashes between Vietnam and Kampuchea resulted in support

Another F-6 of the Somali Aeronautical Corps (SAC) abandoned at Mogadishu along with an AN-24 and several Agusta-Bell AB-205 helicopters. The camouflage was similar to that carried on Chinese F-6s. (Paul Jackson)

for the Pol Pot regime by the Chinese government. In 1977, sixteen F-6s were delivered in crates to Kompong Chnang airfield, the first supersonic fighters of the newly formed Khmer Rouge Air Force. For some reason, only six were assembled and made air worthy, while the rest were still in their crates when Hanoi's invaded Kampuchea. Most Khmer Rouge military equipment was taken to Vietnam, including the crated F-6s. In the Summer of 1980 a few Vietnamese Air Force F-6s were operational at Siem Riep airfield in Kampuchea and at least six of these were subsequently transferred to the Cambodian Air Force.

By far the largest operator of the F-6 outside China is the Democratic People's Republic of Korea (North Korea) which has an inventory of over 100 Farmer Cs. Initially placed in interceptor regiments they were subsequently allocated to ground support units once MiG-23s and MiG-29s became available to North Korea.

The F-6 was in the inventories of both combatants in the Iran/Iraq war. Forty F-6s were supplied to Iraq from Egyptian Air Force stocks during 1983. The Iraqi Air Force used the F-6 in the ground support role but in general preferred rotary winged platforms (such as the Mi 24 Hind) for this duty. As a result, most F-6s were used for training and as a reserve force based at Rashid, Amarah, Karbala and Jalibah. During Operation DESERT STORM Iraqi Air Force F-6s saw no combat against coalition forces.

The Islamic Republic of Iran reportedly received twenty-four F-6s from North Korean stocks. These were delivered aboard a North Korean ship during April of 1983. The F-6s were mainly used in the air defense role by the Islamic Republic of Iran Air Force (IRIAF). Technical support and spare parts for the IRIAF F-6s was supplied by Syria, Pakistan and China.

Numerically the most important user of the F-6 in the Middle East is Egypt. After the country cut its close links with the Soviet Union during 1976, it established contacts with the People's Republic of China. As a result of trade agreements, a number of F-6s were delivered. No. 242 Brigade at Beni Suef was equipped with the F-6s, followed by No. 241 Brigade at Bielbeis East Air Base. A number of Egyptian F-6s have been locally modified to carry the French Matra Magic air-to-air missile.

Because of its very favorable price and purchase agreements, the F-6 has became very popular in Third World countries, especially on the African continent. The United Republic of Tanzania received twelve F-6s during 1974. These aircraft were used to equip one of the three air defense squadrons were based at Mikumi. During 1977, Zambia received twelve F-6s which serve alongside F-5s (MiG-17F) and MiG-21MFs as part of the Zambian Air Defense Command. The Farmers are assigned to two mixed air defense/ground attack squadrons (F-6/F-5). Sudan received nine F-6s to bolster their ground support squadron. These aircraft also serve alongside F-5s and MiG-21s forming one of the three fighter squadrons in the Sudanese Air Force.

The Somali Democratic Republic received its first F-6s after the 1977-78 border war with Ethiopia. During this war, more than half of the entire ***Dayuuradaha Xoogga Dalka Somaliyeed*** (Somali Aeronautical Corps) had been lost. Most of the F-6s delivered came from production Batch 105 along with a few from Batch 106. They were built in China alongside F-6s destined for Pakistan. The first were shipped by vessel to Somalia in 1980. All Somali F-6s carry three digit Black tactical numbers in the 400 range. The camouflage applied to most of the aircraft consisted of a pattern of Yellow-Brown, Earth Brown and Light Green on the uppersurfaces over Light Blue undersurfaces. A serious shortage of spare parts forced the Aeronautical Corps to scrap a number of their Farmers in order to keep others air worthy. When the first U.S. Marines arrived in Somalia in December of 1992 in order to restore order they found a number of F-6s in unserviceable conditions at Mogadishu and Hargeisa. This was the result of two years of anarchy, when armed gangs looted just about anything in Somalia which was not set in concrete.

The sole F-6 operator in Europe the People's Socialist Republic of Albania. In 1961, President Enver Hoxha switched the country's political ties from the Soviets to China. After this, most military equipment received by Albania came from the PRC. The first twelve F-6s arrived during 1965 in the exchange for a like number of MiG-19PM originally received from the Soviet Union.

Albania received a total of three batches, for a total of seventy aircraft. These arrived by sea until 1978, when a political split developed between Albania and the PRC. Albania now faces a situation of being completely cut off from the flow of spare parts from the People's Republic of China. The ***Forcat Ushtarake Ajore Shgipetare*** (Albanian Air Force) was able to obtain a number of engines and airframe parts from various other sources. The WP-6 engines are overhauled every 100 hours, the airframe every 600 hours at the Aviation Maintenance Unit at Kucova.

Most Albanian F-6s are early models without the braking parachute container at the base of the rudder. The first digit of the tactical number on Albanian F-6s denotes the Regiment that the aircraft is assigned to. There were three units equipped with the F-6; Regiment 1875 at Berat-Kucove (4), Regiment 5646 (8) at Lezha-Zadrima and Regiment 7594 (3) at Tirana-Rinas. Since no FT-6 trainers were delivered transition training is accomplished using the MiG-15UTI or the FT-5.

With the fall of the Communist Regime under Ramiz Alia in 1990 the Albanian Air Force national marking was reportedly changed from a Orange Star in a Black circle into a Red rectangle with a Black two headed eagle.

JJ-6/FT-6 Trainer

JJ-6 Trainer

There was no two seat trainer version of the MiG-19 Farmer developed and built in the Soviet Union. From time to time a picture of a so-called MiG-19UTI with the fuselage number 6 appeared in various Western magazines and books; however, this was a hoax. An Eastern bloc aviation enthusiast, who initially wanted to became famous and to earn money, supplied the pictures of the "MiG-19UTI" to the West. The original picture was of the SM-9/3 prototype, which was retouched and given an additional canopy, as well another tactical. Due to the generally bad quality and the censoring of photos in Soviet books and magazines no one in the West doubted the photos, in fact, a two seat version of the MiG-19 never existed!

Although normal Soviet doctrine was to produce a two seat trainer variant of most single seat fighters, it was normal to expect the development of a MiG-19UTI. Since the Soviets viewed the MiG-19 as an interim aircraft pending the arrival of the more advanced MiG-21, it was decided not to proceed with development of a two seat MiG-19.

Conversion training for Soviet and Warsaw Pact pilots was undertaken on the MiG-15UTI Midget and for pilot destined to fly MiG-19P and PM variants training was conducted on the single seat MiG-17PF to familiarize them with the operation of the RP-2U and RP-5 radar systems.

In the People's Republic of China the J-6 was the backbone of the air defense units of the People's Liberation Army and the military services urgently needed a trainer to allow pilots to quickly transition from the F-5 (MiG-17F) to the J-6. What was needed was an aircraft with

The only FT-6, Black 902, allocated to No 15 Squadron, Cobras, at Peshawar Air Base, Pakistan. This overall White FT-6 has Red checkers applied to the nose and rudder. Additionally, the tips of the underwing 200 gallon (760 liter) drop tanks are in Red. (Peter Steinemann)

This FT-6, Black 10117, belongs to No 19 Squadron at Marsoor. The antenna on the port side of the nose is a Pakistani modification done in-country during routine overhaul. Although the aircraft is camouflaged in a pattern and colors similar to that carried on Pakistani F-16s, the two 200 gallon underwing tanks are in Natural Metal. (Peter Steinemann)

Fuselage Development

Shenyang J-6/F-6 (Late)

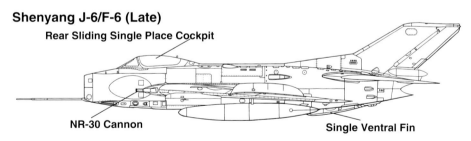

Shenyang JJ-6/FT-6

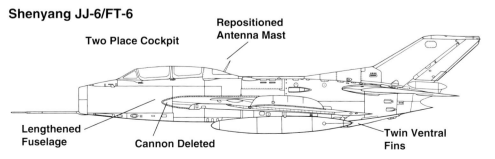

55

This FT-6, Black 106, belongs to the No 19 Squadron at Marsoor and carries the unit's Yellow and Black unit insignia on the fin. The TF-6 has no wing root cannons of under-wing AIM-9 Sidewinder missile pylons. The two drop tanks are Natural Metal with Red tips. (Peter Steinemann)

similar performance to the J-6.

In October of 1966, some five years after production of the J-6 begun at Shenyang, the Ministry of Aviation Industry approved a design proposal submitted by the Shenyang Aircraft Design Institute for a two seat trainer variant of the J-6 to be designated the JJ-6 (Jianjiji Jiaolianji or Fighter-Trainer).

Experience gained during the development of the JJ-5 (a Chinese trainer version of the

This is the only FT-6, Black 10836, assigned to No 26, Spider, Squadron at Peshawar. This is an A-5 Fantan attack unit, and has an FT-6 on strength as a conversion/proficiency trainer. The TF-6 canopy differs from the F-6 canopy in that both FT-6 opens to starboard, while the F-6 canopy is a rear sliding type. (Peter Steinemann)

This overall White FT-6, Black 332, belongs to the No 25 Squadron, Bangladeshi Air Force. The aircraft once served with the Pakistani Air Force, the source of most F-6/TF-6s in the Bangladeshi inventory. The large Black tactical number on the nose is unusual. (Peter Steinemann)

MiG-17 Fresco) was used to speed up the development of the JJ-6 and during 1967 work was started on the prototype. On 6 November 1970, some four years after the proposal was approved, the prototype JJ-6 took off for its first flight.

Series production of the JJ-6 was started during December of 1973, and a total of 634 JJ-6 were produced between 1973 and 1986. A number of these being exported to client nations operating the F-6 fighter and A-5 Fantan attack aircraft.

There were a number of differences between the J-6 fighter and the JJ-6 trainer. The fuselage was lengthened by two feet nine inches to make room for the second cockpit. The installation of the second cockpit resulted in a larger dorsal spine and while the canopy of the J-6 slides to the rear, the two canopies of the JJ-6 both open to starboard. The two cockpits are separated by a glass screen and each has their own individual pressurization systems. By using this method, there is no loss of cabin pressure in the second cockpit should one of the canopies be lost. The front cockpit controls are automatically disconnected whenever the instructor in the rear cockpit took control. The communications intercom system used on the JJ-6 is a Chinese version of the Soviet SPU-2P intercom.

The antenna mast, located on the starboard side below the canopy was relocated to the center of the dorsal spine behind the rear canopy.

As a weight saving measure, the two NR-30 wing root cannons were deleted along with their gun blast panels, while the nose mounted cannon was retained for weapons training. JJ-6 has the same gunsight and weapons related avionics as the single seat fighter.

There are two small ventral fins, one on either side of the original large ventral centerline fin. These were added to improve directional stability which was adversely affected by the increased length of the JJ-6 fuselage. All JJ-6s have the drag parachute container at the base of the rudder and are equipped with the forward wing leading edge pylon.

Not only was the JJ-6 used for conversion training for pilots destined for J-6 squadrons, it

An overall White FT-6, Black 840, of the No 25 Squadron at Chittagong-Patenga Air Base, Bangladesh. The wing pylon was Natural Metal and the air intake lip was in Red was was the tips of both 760 liter drop tanks. The FT-6 serves in both, F-6 and A-5C units within the Bangladesh Air Force. (Peter Steinemann)

This abandoned Somali Aeronautical Corps (SAC) FT-6, Black 405, was found by U.S. Marines on the Mogadishu Airport scrap dump in December of 1992. The F-6 has camouflage consisting of Sand-Brown, Earth-Brown, Light-Green and Medium Green over Light Blue undersurfaces. (Paul Jackson)

was also used to train pilots for the Q-5 (A-5) Fantan attack aircraft. JJ-6s continue to be assigned to Q-5 regiments for proficiency training.

Export FT-6 Trainer

The JJ-6 was delivered to a number of client states under the export designation FT-6 (FT for Fighter Trainer). Externally these aircraft are identical to the Chinese JJ-6 aircraft. FT-6s were delivered from the factory in either overall Natural metal or overall White, although some Pakistani Air Force aircraft were camouflaged.

Pakistani Air Force FT-6s received the same modifications as the F-6s with the exception of the additional pylon for the AIM-9 Sidewinder. The antenna mast, deleted on all Pakistani F-6, was retained on the FT-6s, but the aerial on top of the port side of the nose was also added. As with the F-6, the trainer version also was refitted with British Martin-Baker Mk PKD 10 ejection seats.

Not all customers of the F-6 automatically ordered the FT-6, but most did. For instance, the Albanian Air Force uses the MiG-15UTI and the FT-5 for conversion training to the F6 and has no FT-6s in its inventory.

The FT-6 has also been exported to countries with A-5C attack aircraft in their inventories, namely Bangladesh and Pakistan, both of who took delivery of the A-5 during 1983.

MiG Fighters
From
squadron/signal publications

1116

1125

1131

squadron/signal publications